HAUNTED
DEVON

HAUNTED
DEVON

IAN ADDICOAT

TEMPUS

I would like to dedicate this book to the memory of two very good friends who have both passed away since my last book was published:

Geoff Buswell (1947-2004) with whom I wrote my last book

Alan Maxted (1960-2005) whose enthusiasm for the paranormal was second to none

First published 2006

Tempus Publishing Limited
The Mill, Brimscombe Port,
Stroud, Gloucestershire, GL5 2QG
www.tempus-publishing.com

British Library Cataloguing in Publication Data.
A catalogue record for this book is available from the British Library.

ISBN 0 7524 3977 4

Typesetting and origination by Tempus Publishing Limited.
Printed in Great Britain.

CONTENTS

About the Author   7

Acknowledgements   8

Introduction   9

An A-Z of Haunted Devon   11

Reference/Source Books   94

The unique and atmospheric Highwayman Inn, Sourton.

ABOUT THE AUTHOR

Ian Addicoat is an established writer and researcher of the paranormal. He is president of the Paranormal Research Organisation and has investigated numerous haunted properties, specialising in the South West. He has appeared on various television programmes, including *Most Haunted*, *Animal X* and *GMTV*, and is a partner in two companies specialising in ghost walks and paranormal events. Above all Ian prides himself on his rational approach to ghosts and the supernatural.

ACKNOWLEDGEMENTS

Special thanks to Stuart Andrews and William Brunning: business colleagues in Haunting Experiences and joke sharers but above all magnificent friends. (www.hauntingexperiences. co.uk).

I would like to offer my sincerest thanks to all my good friends and fellow investigators in the Paranormal Research Organisation (UK) for spending the night with me on numerous occasions in the name of paranormal study. (www.paranormalresearch.org.uk).

Fred Moore for his fantastic websites, funny emails and munificent help with computer problems. (www.ghosthunting.org.uk and others).

Kizzy Brown from the Anthony Nolan Trust – a wonderful cause and a generous, warm and very humorous person. (www.anthonynolan.org.uk).

For photographs: all photographs in the book were taken by myself apart from those acknowledged otherwise. Special thanks for this goes to Stuart Andrews, Will Brunning, Kevin Hynes, Shaun Markham, Julien Wilkinson of Abode Hotels and Debbie Lewis of Exeter City Council.

Other Assistance: The Red Coat Guides of Exeter; Steve Bax – English Heritage; Penny – Dartmoor Tourist Association; Alex Duncan – www.sampford-peverell.co.uk; Debbie Moss – www.boringdonhall.co.uk; Noreen Medland – Exeter City Council; Carla, Wheel Farm Guest House, near Ilfracombe, for her warm welcome and delicious breakfast; everyone else who offered stories, anecdotes, etc. Also, of course, all of my friends and family, but the most gratitude has to go to my wife Debbie and my children Alishia and Connor for their patience, understanding, support and love!

INTRODUCTION

Devon is unique and unlike any other county in England; it is even poles apart from its near-neighbour Cornwall. One cannot ignore the dominant ocean, whose exposed and brooding jagged cliffs have savagely wrecked countless ships, and from where fair traders and smugglers have plied their trade; from where the *Mayflower* set sail in search of the New World and from where salty sea dogs such as Sir Francis Drake and Sir Walter Raleigh shaped the very fabric of seafaring legends. Age-old fishing villages, miles of golden sand, busy resorts and naval ports stretch around the coastline.

Moving inland one can discover lively market towns, city centres and time-honoured villages complete with country pubs, real ale and Devonshire cream teas, brimming with Devon Longhouses, ancient stone bridges, thatched cottages and picture-postcard hamlets, and steeped in tradition with unusual folklore, events and customs. Devon has a remarkable and incredible history and heritage with grand cathedrals, majestic grey churches, tranquil abbeys, prehistoric stone circles and dolmen, awe-inspiring castles and fortresses, remarkable manor houses, exquisite Gothic mansions and tales of death, battles and intrigue spreading across the landscape.

There is an untamed and yet wonderful countryside consisting of wild moorland landscapes, woodland, sparkling clear rivers and streams, farmland, patchwork fields, green undulating hills, footpaths and bridleways, lush high-sided lanes, and deep sylvan and secluded valleys to explore. Oh yeah, there are also ghosts, myths and legends!

One cannot realistically visit Devon without hearing stories of Hairy Hands, Black Dogs, spectral monks, unearthly footsteps and an array of ethereal encounters. It is a county of folklore and ghostlore, mystery and murder, intrigue and curiosity. Indeed it seems to have more than its fair share of haunted locations and the paranormal seems to come bursting out of every corner. The legends have inspired such authors as Sir Arthur Conan Doyle, R.D. Blackmore and Agatha Christie, and many films and television programmes have been filmed in the Devon countryside. However, beyond the legends there does appear to be a streak of reality to the ghostly shenanigans which encompass Devon.

I have always lived in the West Country, and have visited and stayed in countless haunted locations. I have sometimes been left with a feeling of an altogether unexplained ambience. While I class myself as still sceptical of ghost stories (a sceptic in the true sense – questioning not blinkered) there are still things which are unexplained. The stories and accounts in this book are not meant to offer any proof or overwhelming evidence; indeed, I feel that that is not something that could be presumed by such a book. However, I have attempted to provide fresh knowledge and personal accounts of new and traditional stories. Enjoy the book, and visit as many of the places as you can, for two reasons; firstly, because Devon is inspirational and one cannot fail but to enjoy its splendour, and secondly, because only by visiting such places and spending time there can you truly get a fuller picture of them, and you never know, you might just have your very own experience of the paranormal.

Happy ghost hunting!

Ian Addicoat

AN A-Z OF HAUNTED DEVON

Ashburton

Bay Horse Inn

This is a friendly, popular and traditional pub situated in North Street. It is said that the haunting manifestation here is related to a child (or, perhaps, children). In the past, various unexplainable sounds have been heard, including the unmistakeable noises of small running footsteps when no child could actually be present. Other peculiar noises heard here have included the melancholy resonance of a sobbing girl. Tradition has it that this was a youngster who caught diphtheria and died in this building. There appears to be less activity now than in previous years. The pub does, however, retain an atmosphere which is almost palpable.

Kutty (Cutty) Dyer

Ashburton itself is a former stannary town and was a popular stopping-off place for sailors from Dartmouth. For many years a local legend has claimed that 'Kutty Dyer', a water sprite, haunts the town and resides near the King's Bridge. The fable tells how this evil 'fairy' would frequently pay visits to mischievous children or drunks and then either throw them in the River Ashburn or commit the far more heinous crime of slitting their throats and drinking their blood; an all-round charmer it seems!

I remember on my last visit to Ashburton my companion was suddenly gripped by a strong feeling of melancholy as we walked up North Street towards the pub. She had certainly not known the story or ever visited the area before, though I have come to believe her 'psychic' impressions. What she was linking into is impossible to say, but it was certainly a potent experience for her, and indeed, for myself, observing her behaviour.

Bay Horse Inn, Ashburton.

Berry Pomeroy

Castle

Castles rarely fail to disappoint you when you're on a quest for a good ghost story and Berry Pomeroy, near Totnes, is certainly no exception. It is inundated with tales of terror and supernatural encounters, and rarely fails to get a mention whenever a new ghost book materialises! The castle itself has had a long and varied history, from its time as a Saxon manor to the current building, which is in near ruin. The De la Pomerais family owned it until 1548, and later the Seymour clan, Dukes of Somerset, possessed it. By the late seventeenth century the castle was almost deserted, but it is still owned by the Duke of Somerset and is maintained by English Heritage.

The tales of ghosts and the paranormal are quite extraordinary; people experience overwhelming fear, hostility and dark atmospheres, strange lights, smells and sounds. Animals often act very strangely, people may feel the touch of an unseen hand or even a shove, cameras and other equipment fail, and there have been numerous sightings of ghostly figures. These include: the White Lady: believed to be Lady Margaret Pomeroy, who was imprisoned in the dungeon by her jealous sister Eleanor.

Berry Pomeroy (kindly provided by Kevin Hynes).

The Blue Lady: seen wringing her hands in great distress. She is thought to be a baron's daughter. Victim of his incestuous urges, she fell pregnant. She strangled the newborn baby and subsequently haunts the site as a supposed harbinger of death.

The Black Hound: a classic Devon black dog story of a creature said to appear as a portent.

Isabelle: the presence of a nine-year-old girl, the illegitimate child of Baron de Pomeroy, who was confined to the castle. She was allegedly murdered whilst trying to save her mother from being raped.

Other phenomena: time slips and the ghosts of an old man carrying a scythe, a quaint old lady, a small hooded boy, a sullen girl, an Elizabethan figure seen at a window with a white ruffle, a man in Stuart costume, a face at the gatehouse window, a cavalier and a crying baby, the sound of footsteps and heavy falls, the smell of perfume, doors slamming, hoof beats, camera films becoming blank – and so much more.

Berry Pomeroy (kindly provided by Kevin Hynes).

Sightings are reported to have happened for at least 200 years and are still regularly occurring today, making Berry Pomeroy a leading candidate to be Britain's most haunted castle. My good friends Kevin Hynes and Stuart Andrews carried out an investigation here with a team from Devon in Spring 2006. I have included with kind permission a copy of Kevin's report summary:

Seymour Building
Through dowsing I picked up on the following information:

Kitchen Area
Female One:
Happy to communicate with us and aware she has passed. Passed in 1685 aged thirty-four years, cause of death was heart related.
Female Two:
This female was also happy to communicate; she had lived here in the building when she was alive. Through dowsing I was also able to get her name, which was Isabelle.
Male One:
Once again this presence was happy to communicate and was aware he had passed. He passed

in 1785 aged thirty-one: cause of death was disease. He had worked in the building when he was alive. He was married with two children.

Male Two:
This male presence was aware he had passed and was also happy to communicate. He passed in 1684 aged thirty-five. He was murdered (stabbed). This male had also worked here when alive.

Elizabethan Great Hall
Through dowsing I again picked up on the presence of a male. He had passed in 1414 aged fourteen: the cause of death was an accident. In one particular area a warm spot was picked up. I dowsed to find out what was causing this and picked up on the presence of Isabelle, the female from earlier. The team asked various questions and we found that she was following us around and was interested in what we were doing. I also picked up on a ley line in this area of the Seymour Building.

The Chapel
In the main chapel area, once again through dowsing, I picked up on the following presences: three males, one female, and a negative energy. The female presence was Isabelle: she was keeping true to her word and following the team around. One of the male presences was inside the enclosed wooded area of the room: he passed in 1674 and the cause of death was an accident. During the time I was carrying out dowsing for this male I had a very tight pain in my chest area, which I mentioned to the rest of the team. This only seemed to last for a short while.

The team did manage to capture a number of anomalies both on still and night-vision camera:

Towers
The team also investigated the two towers either side of the main entrance; there was a definite change in atmosphere in the two towers. The one on the right, as you look at the building from the outside, felt very calming and quiet, whereas the other tower, on the left-hand side, felt very oppressive and unwelcoming; one member of the team and myself felt a sensation as if we were being pulled downwards into the ground. Also, another member seemed to be having trouble keeping her balance, whilst another was feeling a very warm sensation on her back.

Margaret's Tower
Through dowsing I picked up on two female presences. Once again Isabelle had followed us. The other female presence was Margaret. The team carried out a group séance within the tower. Cold spots and breezes were felt by most of the team. Also some of the team felt as if they had been touched. Another member of the team and myself thought we saw a shadow movement out of the corner of our eyes on the stairs. Also, whilst asking for a sign, pretty much on cue, the wind seemed to pick up and the gust a lot stronger.

Conclusion
A very enjoyable investigation at a remarkable venue, with some interesting results picked up.

Brixham.

Brixham

Brixham is a very old and historic town, full of legends and ghosts. Anyone wanting an overview of the haunted heritage of Brixham simply must get hold of a copy of Graham Wyley's *The Ghosts of Brixham*.

Berry Head Fort

Ancient bones and skeletons have been discovered in the area and strange human cries and voices have been heard here. There is also a council house nearby where poltergeist activity has at times been widespread; several different residents have, in fact, been so unnerved by the activity that they have swiftly moved out. Finally, the fort itself may have been the location for the sighting of the ghost of one of history's most famous characters – Emperor Napoleon Bonaparte. After his surrender in 1815 his ship was anchored off Berry Head and, though he never actually came ashore, his ghost was apparently witnessed here on the day of his death. The unmistakeable form of the so-called 'Badinguet' was seen marching along in familiar hat and with right arm characteristically tucked into his tunic. The witness observed him for a short time but before long he simply faded away.

The Black House

Dating from the fourteenth century and possibly built by monks, the Black House is a notoriously haunted building. There have been reports of strange lightning effects in certain rooms and doors locking and unlocking by themselves. A lot of ghostly noises have also been heard, the most common of which is the sound of footsteps and a horse's hoof beats outside. An apparition, believed to be that of sixteenth-century Squire Hilliard, is sometimes seen at an upstairs window.

Overgang, Brixham.

Overgang

Brixham is famous for being the landing spot of William III of Orange, who arrived with his Dutch army on 5 November 1688. Many a local 'Brixhamite' still bears a Dutch moniker today, being a direct descendant of the 20,000 landed soldiers. Overgang, Dutch for 'a way through or along which someone or something may pass', is where the Dutch marched from the harbour before encamping on the hill above.

People in a particular cottage here have witnessed 'people' walking through the cottage and a dark shrouded man has also been seen in a particular room. A medium believed this to be a man named 'John' who was just walking through.

Pring's Court

Captain Pring was an influential mariner in the town during the nineteenth century and lived in a cottage here (then called Pomeroy Court). The cottages were built in the late eighteenth century, and were at some stage renamed after the captain. They are also rumoured to have been the frequent of many a Brixham smuggler, carrying their contraband through the buildings. A ghostly figure has been seen in the early hours loitering in a corridor of one cottage. One former resident walked straight through the shade and described an exceptionally icy temperature. Voices have also been heard in the particular cottage where Pring himself lived for many years. In another cottage here, the ghost of Roger Pomeroy (descendant of the Pomeroys of Berry Pomeroy Castle) is also said to trouble the residents on occasions.

Pring's Court, Brixham.

St Mary's Churchyard

The main church in the town is St Mary's, and it is the third to have been built on the site, which was an ancient Celtic burial ground. The original wooden Saxon church was replaced by a stone Norman one and the current church was built in about 1360. Many of Brixham's former residents are buried in the churchyard, and it said that nobody can lay claim to be a true 'Brixhamite' until they have at least three generations of ancestors buried in the churchyard here. It is deemed extremely unlucky to walk anticlockwise around the church.

Nearby Lichfield Drive (from the Anglo-Saxon *lich*, meaning a corpse) was the route that the dead were taken along for burial at St Mary's churchyard. Many people have described feelings akin to 'being in ancient times' whilst in the churchyard; other folk describe a sense of a 'power' or a 'strong energy'. This may perhaps be because there is said to be a very powerful ley line running through this particular church.

The Smuggler's Haunt Inn

Set in a truly beautiful Devon coastal town, the Smuggler's Haunt Inn, just a stone's throw away from the harbour, claims to possess a few resident ghosts. This was another location visited by *Most Haunted* during one of their live shows. The inn has a notorious history of smuggling but nowadays it is well known for its ghosts, with many documented accounts of sightings and paranormal events. Guests as well as owners, past and present, have witnessed strange phenomena here. Indeed according to my colleague, Richard Jones, the Torquay police force has a whole documented file on record relating to the ghostly shenanigans at this 300-year-old inn. Even some of the most sceptical of people have walked away very puzzled as a result of their experiences during their stay at this wonderfully atmospheric hostelry.

Smugglers Haunt, Brixham (kindly provided by Shaun Markham).

In February 2006 we organised a charity event with Haunting Experiences to raise money for the Anthony Nolan Trust, and had an amazing night. After the team had assembled we enjoyed a three-course meal before dividing into four investigation groups. These groups remained constant for most of the night, rotating to different areas within the oldest parts of the building, with a different guide for each session. The team leaders were Stuart Andrews, Will Brunning, Kevin Hynes and myself. We were also privileged to be accompanied by Kizzy Brown from the Anthony Nolan Trust and Fred Moore and Shaun Markham, who are Haunting Experience's IT consultants, and we were grateful for their invaluable assistance during this intriguing night.

Before the investigation began we were able to take a brief tour of the areas of the hotel we would be focusing on for the night. This was invaluable in terms of familiarising ourselves with the layout of the building and gaining some further knowledge of the reputed activity so that we were able to indicate to our guests when they were near the mark in terms of any previously reported phenomenon. However, we naturally did not share any information until after the teams had investigated the areas concerned.

Rooms One and Two

Room one is believed to be a place where a child was placed in the chimney and died there. Knocking noises are often heard, and guests have frequently captured light anomalies on camera. In room two a medium picked up on the name Agnes. Many locals do talk about the ghost of young 'Aggie', who was a girl who allegedly jumped to her death from an upstairs window some seventy or eighty years ago. The room has now gone; the window would be where the utility room now is.

During the vigils in this room the groups separately picked up through dowsing on a male and a female presence. Intriguingly, one dowser picked up on a teenage girl who claimed she had lived here in the hotel and died of a tragic accident; falling out of a window. Some interesting light anomalies were caught on both night vision and digital cameras in the most relevant areas. Towards the end of one vigil here, everyone present heard what sounded like a knock on the door as if someone wanted to enter; nobody was there and everyone was accounted for.

Several different people, in different teams, said that that they didn't like the chimney area. In room two the presence of a lady named Edith was detected. She was possibly old and had visited here on holiday with her husband when alive. She had apparently died within the last year and had often come to Brixham and the hotel before this. The last time she stayed had been over five years ago, and her husband had been called Charles.

Room Six

A wedding dress has been seen in this room in a cupboard; it is apparently not a real one, but an apparition! Through dowsing, three presences were picked up: two males and a female. One was a man in his thirties named Darren, who was unmarried and had no children. He was apparently murdered, though not in this room. He had been a free trader and had been killed in the 1900s by a fellow smuggler in an argument over contraband. He apparently moves around and makes noises. He was not local or born in Brixham but was actually Cornish. He was buried at Berry Head. He also shot somebody in his past.

At this stage a very high EMF reading was found over the bed, and it seemed to follow one particular lady around the room. When anybody else took the meter it stopped but when returned to the lady's hands it would begin to fluctuate again. She had no obvious electrical equipment so this was a mystery. Even stranger, when I joked that she had 'pulled' (and she replied that she 'already had two men in her life') the readings ceased! During this time several orbs were caught on night-shot video camera.

The group carried out a darkness vigil with all the equipment turned off to see if the presence would communicate with us, and noises were heard from behind the closed bathroom door.

A couple of the group members felt as if they had been touched by something. The group continued to sit quietly, with linked hands, and I actually felt as if someone had touched my ear; this seemed to last for a few minutes.

Various members of the group felt sick and light-headed; people also felt tingling sensations moving around the circle. After the last of the rotated sessions I joined Kevin's group in here, as activity had been apparently widespread. I was directed to sit in a particular area and felt a very strong 'tickling/tingling' on both my neck and ear. I have never experienced anything quite so definitive and hard to explain in all my time at 'haunted' locations. During the last part of the evening, when people were free to return to experience their areas of choice again, I returned here with a group and Kevin to try to carry out a séance. At first I led the proceedings and little occurred but after a while Kevin took over. During this period I was again sat in the back left corner (as before) and once again experienced similar sensations. These feelings began on my shoulder and then on my face. At one stage they stopped and without any prompting from me the lady to my right suddenly exclaimed that she was feeling the same. After a while her experiences ceased and it started on me again. The sensations moved from my right, across my body and began moving down my left arm. Suddenly they ceased and then Kevin (to my left) began feeling a tingling on top of his head. When they left him a lady further along felt sick, another felt tingling and then two others felt tightness in their chest and sickness. Then finally a man (a sceptic) began to feel faint and almost passed out. At this stage I naturally put a halt to proceedings and we made sure he was all right, which I'm glad to say he was. I have never experienced anything quite like this and still find much of it hard to explain. Autosuggestion/mass hysteria and psychology just didn't seem enough to explain such extraordinary events!

Room Seven

Lots of peculiar things allegedly happen in here; light bulbs blow, television sets are mysteriously turned on despite being unplugged, fire doors open and the kettle has been played with. The owner was once sitting on a chest in this room when she was physically shaken; guests have seen an old lady sitting in a rocking chair (no such chair is there now). I was expecting some form of activity in this room, as both staff and the owner had experienced abnormal activity. However, very little happened and the entire group felt this room to be calm and welcoming.

There was a small temperature and EMF irregularity in the vicinity of the radiator, but this was not really of significance and is presumed to have been natural. EMF analysis also showed a high reading and was picked up near to the window area. In a darkness vigil, orbs were captured in front of Kizzy on night vision, and also a strange noise was heard by the whole group which sounded like marbles knocking together.

Room Seventeen

In this room a medium had previously picked up on a smuggler who was seen 'stuffing' things into the attic above. This is interesting because there is no attic now and it has a flat roof! Some suggest this may link with the famous smuggler Bob Elliott who is said to have owned the building in the past (then one of two cottages). He is infamous because of a time where he is said to have evaded capture by customs officers by faking his own death and spiriting his contraband away in his coffin – coming to be known as Resurrection Bob for his antics. Later that day, after his fellow smugglers rescued him from his grave, he was spotted locally by the revenue men, who, as a result believed they'd seen a ghost!

During the vigil, one member of the group felt slightly uneasy and very cold. There were also some sudden drops in temperature (by a couple of degrees), which were picked up by the laser thermometer. A few draughts were felt and there appeared to be no obvious source for these. Also they were not consistent. Another member of the group felt that something was touching him whilst he lay on the bed. One lady had an image in her mind's eye of three women standing beside the bed on the right-hand side, looking down at a male who was dying in the bed.

Just as one group were leaving and had switched the lights back on, the Negative Ion Detector went off the scale and continued to show a high reading for nearly a minute. In the years that we have been investigating using this piece of equipment, this is the first time a reading of this level and length of duration has been recorded. Many believe a change in the ion count within a room indicates a possible spirit presence.

A very interesting room and some very interesting results too! The team picked up on a small girl presence aged around five or six with the initials K.H. Very strange EMF readings were recorded in the place where she said she was standing, only for them to then completely disappear. In conjunction with this the temperature fell from twenty degrees centigrade to fourteen almost instantly. We tried different experiments to try and communicate with her, and using night vision and EVP recording we gathered some amazing results. Orbs seemed to appear on command on night-vision camera with some flashing anomalies, and at one stage an orb

Smugglers Haunt, Brixham.

was captured on video camera moving above the bed. This coincided with a two degree drop in temperature in the same area.

One of our guests caught a very strange EVP of a young girl saying 'one...two...three' as they were trying to communicate with what had been previously discovered to be a little girl. One member of the team felt that an area to the right of the bed and across the room was strange. He had a peculiar feeling about it that he couldn't shake off. A lady picked up on a male presence in the chair and both a man and later a lady in the group did feel odd here. Dowsing revealed a man who had been hanged in the 1600s.

Restaurant

In this area a man has previously been seen at a table – usually in the mirror. He is described as in his forties, wearing a cloth cap, a long raincoat, and with long hair. A man has been seen walking through the bar, and both pipe smoke and perfume have been smelt there. The man in the raincoat has also been seen in the large mirror on the far wall. The kitchens are also said to be very active, and on one occasion a chef was covered in cream after 'taking the Mick' out of the ghost, and many objects have been found to have been moved in the vicinity. Unfortunately, on the night, nothing at all unusual was reported in this area!

Conclusion

An excellent night was had by all, and everybody who attended came away with something to remember. Indeed it was a very eventful night for many of our guests, which we must add, was a good balance of believers, non-believers and those in-between. I look forward to our next visit to this lovely hotel to compare the findings from the two nights and wish to thank all those who attended the night and the fund-raisers for doing such a fine job raising money for such a deserving charity – the Anthon Nolan Trust – and the staff and owners of the Smuggler's Haunt for being such great hosts. For more details, visit www.hauntingexperiences.co.uk.

Buckfast Abbey.

Buckfast

Abbey

Now home to an order of Roman Catholic Benedictine monks, the abbey is said to be haunted by pre-Reformation monks, who have been seen many times in their familiar whitish grey robes – possibly Cistercian monks from the twelfth century. These were particularly frequently sighted in Victorian times, long before the present-day monks returned and when the former medieval abbey lay in ruins. One of these ghosts is believed to be a former abbot who haunts the area of Abbot's Lane. In 1872 a youth out fishing in the river observed a long procession of monks moving towards the abbey. He said the phantoms were completely soundless and was very unnerved by his experience.

In 2002 archaeological excavations revealed what are possibly Anglo-Saxon burials and the foundations of a possible earlier church inside the walls of the medieval area. It is possible that this was an early Christian church – the forerunner to the later Buckfast Abbey?

Buckfastleigh

Holy Trinity Church

Now we are really talking about the stuff of legends – Squire Richard Cabell, quite possibly the inspiration for Sir Arthur Conan Doyle's *Hound of the Baskervilles*. This so-called evil gent was a notorious local villain who scared everyone around Buckfastleigh half to death during the seventeenth century and lived at nearby Brook Manor. Many stories were put forward that he was a vampire, or an evil wrongdoer who had sold his soul to the cloven-hoofed one so he could continue his wickedness. This malevolence was said to include locking up local girls so he could

Buckfastleigh church Steps.

Kings Arms, Buckfastleigh.

have his wicked way with them, murdering his wife, Satanic acts and anything else depraved enough to suit his taste for immorality. Renowned as a man deeply in love with hunting, it is claimed that even in death he is fated to continue the chase with a pack of black hounds (possibly the infamous 'wisht' hounds) that rampage across Dartmoor. When he eventually died in 1677, and was buried in the churchyard, they entombed him under an enormous slab of granite and placed this inside an iron-grilled tomb to stop his predicted nightly perambulations. It still stands today as a unique and impressive 'incarceration'. Soon after his internment the hounds were reportedly packed around his tomb baying their unearthly howls. They appear to have arisen with their master as the hunt is now seen in the surrounding area. He is also rumoured to drive a coach up to Brook Manor in early July (he died on 5 July), again led by the hounds, and he himself is said to be a headless phantom. Particularly on stormy nights, Richard Cabell is said to emerge from his sepulchre and head out down the lane and down the church steps before heading for Dartmoor. A local myth also suggests that if you run around Cabell's tomb thirteen (some say seven) times in an anticlockwise direction and stick your finger in the keyhole, it will be bitten by the ghastly Cabell.

In recent times lots of people have claimed to see a peculiar red glow coming from the tomb and others have described strange creatures moving near the area of Cabell's last resting place. I was also interested to hear that there are said locally to be numerous caves underneath the churchyard, and in one of them is said to be a peculiar rock formation which looks exactly like the description of Squire Cabell; it is believed to lie directly beneath his grave. Also in the nineteenth century, it is said, the graveyard's remoteness attracted body snatchers, out of the sight of prying eyes.

When the church was built the Devil (in the true nature of a classic Devon story) is said to have tried to stop its building by moving the stones overnight, but he was apparently foiled by the building of 196 steps. I can honestly say that after walking up them they pretty near foiled me as well.

Sadly the church was burnt down in July 1992 after a fire started in the altar, rumoured to have been the act of a Satanic-minded person, and some say the legend of Cabell has attracted Devil worship here for over a century. Unfortunately, the Cabell family history does not show a single individual who succinctly fits the profile of the story. However it may well be that the legends are an amalgamation of several known Richards and other Cabells from the period.

Kings Arms

This pub was once a coaching hotel and assembly rooms. The building has also been used as a wool factory, seed merchants and headquarters for the nearby racecourse, and as the premises for Kingcombe Sofas. It is believed to be haunted by a classic Grey Lady ghost, complete with long old-fashioned dress. She frequents an area on the staircase where, it is believed, she awaits the return of a lover.

Buckland Abbey.

Buckland

Abbey

This beautiful 700-year-old building has a majestic sixteenth-century great hall, which contains a disconcerting frieze illustrating the peculiar ideas of previous owner, the famed Sir Richard Grenville, and beautiful glass panels commemorating the successes over the Spanish Armada in the stairwell. Indeed, the estate was owned by Elizabethan seafarers Sir Francis Drake and the Grenvilles. Sited in a secluded and peaceful valley, the abbey was home to a Cistercian order of monks until the dissolution of the monasteries, when Henry VIII sold it to Sir Richard Grenville. An old barn dating from those times still lies in the estate and there is an atmosphere of monastic life still falling prevalent over the lands.

Most of the attested stories relate to Sir Francis Drake, and must surely be considered little more than legend? Firstly, it is said that his improvements to the house were ably assisted by the Devil himself. Drake is often claimed to have sold his soul to the Devil in exchange for various rewards, including success in battle. As atonement for this service Drake is fated to force a team of headless horses to drive a jet-black hearse, chased by similarly headless black hounds (what else in Devon?). This occurs in the grounds of Buckland Abbey and the surrounding countryside.

The second legend refers to Drake's Drum – which is said to beat whenever England is in crisis and in need of Drake's service, and many claim it did exactly this during both World Wars and on the eve of the Battle of Trafalgar. The drum now lies in the museum here at Buckland Abbey.

However, if any essence of the past does remain at Buckland Abbey it seems more likely to be some remnants of former monastic life. Peace and tranquillity rule at Buckland, and the atmosphere of serenity is almost tangible. A few people visiting the abbey have claimed to hear Latin chants and 'exquisite' singing.

Cadbury

Fursdon Manor

This is a stylish manor house about two miles from Bickleigh. It has been the family home of the Fursdon family almost continuously since 1259. They have therefore lived here for well over 700 years, apart from a small break in the 1940s when they were forced to move out due to mounting inheritance tax. This single event is believed to have led to the property being haunted by the ghost of Grace Fursdon, who lived here during the reign of Charles I. She is said to have been a formidable lady when in residence and perhaps remains the same after death. When the Fursdons moved out and another family moved in, ghostly activity became almost unbearable, until eventually after twenty years the Fursdons moved back in 1968. They have been there ever since, restoring the property to the grandiosity of former times. However, after I contacted the present owners I was informed that paranormal activity has now abated, perhaps because Grace is content now that the Fursdons are back in residence?

Chagford

The Globe Inn

At the time of writing, this inn has new owners and incorporates a lounge bar, public bar and a function room on the ground floor, with a cobbled courtyard outside. The property also has accommodation rooms, an office, meeting room, private games room and owners' accommodation. There is also a separate cottage with three bedrooms, a bathroom, an open-plan kitchen/diner and a lounge. This was a former coaching inn, still apparently haunted by the troubled soul of a former chambermaid who worked here in the seventeenth century. Local legend claims she was drowned in a witch-test after a wicked local accused her of being in league with Satan. The test proved her innocence but was little compensation as it apparently failed to save her from death and eternal wanderings in the pub.

Globe Inn, Chagford.

Ring O' Bells, Chagford.

St Michael's church, Chagford.

Ring O' Bells Pub

Reported poltergeist activity seems to abound at this hostelry, a charming pub with a warm, welcoming atmosphere. However the activity seems to be mischievous rather than sinister. On many occasions, noises have been heard coming from the cellars when nobody can possibly be down in that area. The activity seems to become more prevalent when any upheaval occurs (for example, when a new landlord moves in, or when work is being carried out at the pub).

Three Crowns, Chagford.

St Michael's Church

Chagford's stunning church of St Michael has a fifteenth-century tower and represents some fascinating history. It is believed that the famous story of Lorna Doone, written by R.D. Blackmore and one of the best-selling novels of the nineteenth century, is inspired by events which occurred at this very church. Inside the church is an inscription 'in memory of Mary WHIDDON who died on 11 October 1641'. Mary was a descendant of John Whiddon, who built the Three Crowns building, and she was shot by a jealous former lover, right here on the steps (or as some say, at the altar) of the church. This tragedy happened immediately after her wedding and her sad spirit has been seen both within the churchyard and also at nearby Whiddon Park. She is described as being a sad spectre, wearing a wedding dress of the style of the seventeenth century.

Three Crowns Hotel

This thirteenth-century granite-faceted thatched inn occupies a significant place in the history of Chagford. It has been used as an inn for over a century and has an almost ageless ambience, yet it bustles with an abundance of history. It is magnificent, with distinctive iron-barred mullioned windows, colossal oak beams, a great open fireplace and four-poster bedrooms. The Victorian novelist Charles Kingsley described it as, 'a beautiful old mullioned perpendicular inn'. The building itself was once the home of the Whiddon (Whyddon) family, who lived in Chagford for numerous centuries, and has been visited by a number of well-known persons from history. In February 1643, the Cornish Royalist and court poet Sydney Godolphin is believed to have died a violent death in the hotel's porch after being fatally wounded in a nearby scuffle; such occurrences would have been familiar during the Civil War era. A Parliamentarian soldier shot him with a musket in Chagford; as the conflict raged his dying form was carried here. He then collapsed and died on one of the stone benches before being taken into the building, and was later buried at Okehampton. His luckless ghost is now believed to haunt the inn and surrounding area.

Resplendent in Cavalier's uniform and plumed hat, he appears at various times and in different places, including rooms and corridors, and has even been witnessed walking through walls with a sad countenance perceptible on his face. At other times he seems to make no visible presence but instead people hear heavy booted footsteps. Recently a couple from Paignton were staying here when they sensed someone by the bed; a young lady in a blue dress, possibly Mary Whyddon.

Grounds of Chambercombe Manor, Ilfracombe.

Chambercombe

Manor

The guide leaflet states:

> Reputedly one of the most haunted dwellings in the UK, visitors have witnessed a host of phenomena which cannot be accounted for; the swinging pendulum of a clock without its weights, the spinning of curtain poles and the kitchen spit that does not have to be wound by a living hand. With parts of the existing manor dating as far back as 1066, it comes as no surprise that Chambercombe Manor has ghosts that are definitely still in residence and often let their presence be known. Visitors have reported a feeling of being watched, of being touched by ghosts, and being pushed out of chairs! Dare you take a tour with the manor's guides, who seem to attract the spirits? You never know what you might experience at Chambercombe Manor.

This house, dating from the eleventh century (much of the present one being fifteenth century), is a wonderful example of a Devon manor. It is included in the Domesday Book and was owned successively by the Champernon and Grey (of Lady Jane fame) families until almost the end of the seventeenth century. After this, and for quite some time, it was a farmhouse and alleged centre for smuggling activity. Indeed a tunnel was discovered in Victorian times leading from the beach to the manor. It is now owned by a charitable trust and open to the public, and within the building various historical changes to the structure, staircases and rooms are evident.

Back in the mid-nineteenth century a secret Elizabethan compartment was discovered. Inside was a fully furnished chamber including a four-poster bed, and lying on the bed was the skeleton of a young woman bearing a peculiar grin etched on her 'face', and a bony arm stretched across the faded coverlet. There have been various explanations as to whom this lady was, with some claiming her to be a Spanish noblewoman captured from a wrecked ship, robbed, walled up and left to die. However, another story suggests she may be Kate Oatway, daughter of a local wrecker, who threatened to report him to the local revenue men. To prevent this, her father,

Chambercombe Manor, Ilfracombe (kindly provided by Stuart Andrews).

William, who lived at the manor in the sixteenth or seventeenth century, allegedly murdered her and walled her up in the secret cavity. One story differs by claiming that William Oatway married the wrecked Spanish woman, who was in fact the mother of Kate. Kate later left to live in Ireland and married an Irish sea captain named Wallace; allegedly, on Kate's return, her ship was wrecked and her injured body thrown up onto the beach at nearby Hele. Her father found her, but her injuries were so severe that he failed to recognise her and stole her jewellery. When he later discovered the identity of the body – one Kate Wallace – full of remorse he buried her in the secret room and left Chambercombe forever. The details were apparently found after his death, in papers buried in a wall at his later house in Fowey, Cornwall. The owner of the skeleton is now said to haunt atmospheric Chambercombe, especially the rooms adjacent to the secret one. She is described as a tall lady in grey.

Two little girls are said to haunt the upstairs rooms – especially the Chippendale bedroom. One is said to be an eight-year-old blonde niece of the Vye family who died here of pneumonia in 1700, and the other is a six-year-old who follows guides on house tours. She has long red hair, wears a blue and white Victorian-style dress, is called Aily and carries a dolly. In the Lady Jane Grey room, a crib has been observed to move, and occasionally a baby has been seen here and a lady has been witnessed rocking it. Legend has it that a fourteen-year-old girl called Alice was raped by a servant and had a child.

Quite a few people have been spooked by the place, with mediums, clairvoyants, members of the public and other visitors leaving very quickly, including some previously sceptical guests. They often describe a sudden coldness, tingling, a tug on clothing and other unexplainable sensations, and a particular candlestick and a wooden crown are often found to have moved. A White Lady has been seen near the pond in the grounds. Strangely enough I was here with my friend Stuart one recent Sunday to discuss holding a Haunting Experiences charity night here, later in the year. Before they opened to the general public we took a walk around the grounds. At one particular point we both stated that we felt odd and made a joke of it; we certainly weren't aware of anything previously happening here. However, later on when we were lucky enough to be given a personal tour of the house, we were informed that this spot was exactly where the lady walks – we both gave a wry grin and simply looked at each other knowingly!

*Leigh Manor, Combe
Martin.*

Combe Martin

Higher Leigh Manor

This is now part of the Combe Martin Wildlife & Dinosaur Park and is a fine-looking Victorian manor house built in 1866. It had fallen into dereliction, but it was bought in the 1980s and rejuvenated into its present-day condition. The park itself is home to wolves, birds of prey, snow leopards and many other endangered animals, and a multitude of model dinosaurs. I visited a few years ago with my wife and children and it was a great day out – even when we were covered in water by a gigantic spitting model of a dinosaur. During the late afternoon I wandered alone into the manor house and could find nobody around so began to explore the downstairs rooms. I distinctly recall feeling wary that someone could appear at any moment, and I fully expected to meet someone at any time, unsure if I was supposed to walk around here. I was sure I was not alone and at one stage actually thought I heard approaching footsteps from the stairs. On investigation I could only find a knight in armour (not a real or ghostly one, I hasten to add!).

Eventually I left the area, and soon afterwards a member of staff appeared to close up the building and I soon managed to confirm that I'd been completely alone. Later, when I read the guidebook, I found a page describing the manor house's history and was intrigued to see that it concentrated on ghost stories of which I had not had any previous knowledge, and have since found no other public reference to. Nevertheless, the guidebook claims that the building houses a number of ghosts and people have felt their presence over many years. The experiences have included peculiar lights, noises, 'including footsteps', and figures who have simply disappeared, including one who will not allow people to pass. It is believed that the house may still contain the residual energy of the nuns of the order of Our Lady of the Sacred Heart who used to reside here in the mid-twentieth century. Also, when I later studied the photographs taken during the visit, I discovered all of those in the manor were extremely fuzzy and un-viewable!

Combe Martin church.

St Peter Ad Vincula Church

This red sandstone church is situated on the main road as you enter Combe Martin, approximately a mile into the village, with a small stream adjacent to the churchyard wall. The chancel dates from the thirteenth century, but the rest of the church is mostly fifteenth century, including the ninety-nine foot tower. The southern door of this building has a fascinating sanctuary ring. It is said that criminals who grabbed it would be saved from arrest and imprisonment - as long as they confessed their crimes and left the country. This practice was abolished in the seventeenth century. The church is believed to be haunted by a devout procession. On more than one occasion a large group of people have been witnessed walking down the aisle, headed by what appears to be a bishop. The mysterious party is said to include various religiously-attired men (priests, etc) who look earnest and sober. When they approach the other end of the church the stunned witnesses see them apparently just disappear into thin air.

In the chancel is an unusual old chair, previously used, it is said, by the bishop; it is over 500 years old, and perhaps this is in someway connected to the bishop of the sightings?

Compton

Castle

This is an almost fairy-tale, castle-style, fortified manor house, complete with towers, battlements, an old medieval-style kitchen, spiral staircase, a great hall, a family chapel and charming gardens. The property is situated near Torquay, in south Devon, and was built in 1340 by the Gilbert family (who discovered Newfoundland in the sixteenth century). The Gilberts still reside at the property today, although it is has been owned by the National Trust since 1951.

Compton Castle.

Compton Castle was also one of several local sites used for the 1995 film production of *Sense and Sensibility*.

As for the paranormal, it is not widely known but several people have reported a feeling of being watched in the dungeon areas, accompanied by a sense of anxiety and melancholy. Dennis Bardens wrote about an estate agent who visited here with his greyhound dog. The animal immediately started to act strangely, uncharacteristically cowering as if in terror.

Dartmouth

Castle

Perhaps unexpectedly, there are not many ghost stories attached to this fifteenth-century castle, which dominates the entrance to the Dart Estuary. Built to guard the local merchants, it was the first English fortress to specifically incorporate plans for guns in the design process and marked the emergence of artillery-reinforced castellation. It consists of a round and a square tower, with gun platforms and gun/musket ports around the towers.

Above left: Dartmouth Castle (kindly provided by Stuart Andrews).

Above right: Dartmouth Royal Castle Hotel (kindly provided by Stuart Andrews).

The only apparent paranormal phenomenon incorporates the sounds of shouting and of gunfire, perhaps associated with an attack here during the Civil War in January 1646 when Fairfax and his army laid siege to the castle before eventually taking over Dartmouth.

Royal Castle Hotel

This award-winning seventeenth-century accommodation and former coaching inn is located in the centre of Dartmouth overlooking the Dart Estuary. The hotel has a significant past, the current building being created from two much earlier buildings. The old courtyard between them, where the stagecoaches used to bring in guests, has been cleverly modified to form an open-plan stair system that still retains the character of the original courtyard. The beams in the ceiling of this area are said to come from the wreckage of the galleons of the Spanish Armada. Furthermore, Charles II is said to have stayed here, and other noted guests have apparently included Queen Victoria and Sir Francis Drake.

If you want to experience the supernatural at this seaside hotel, it is recommended you stay during the autumn, as that appears to be when much of the paranormal activity occurs.

The main phenomenon reported at the hotel is the sound of a coach and horses, which are heard arriving outside (though some describe the sound as if the coach is about to come through the foyer, where the original coach entry would have been). This seems to consistently occur at about 2 a.m., and the coach halts before rumbling off again with the distinct sound of horse's hoof beats and carriage wheels on cobbles. This has been happening for many years and has been reported by a wide variety of people, including staff members and guests.

It is claimed that these noises are a ghostly playback of the arrival at Dartmouth of a coach in 1689 sent by William III to collect Mary II. His wife Mary was staying here awaiting his command to join him. She was originally deposited here anticipating that she would join him when he landed at Dartmouth to claim the throne, but he ended up being forced by a storm to land at nearby Brixham instead. The spectacle of men duelling in the courtyard has also been witnessed, and in a particular room several strange occurrences have been noted, including apparent poltergeist activity.

Royal Naval College

This building on Boon Hill is supposedly haunted by Squire Boon, who used to live in a house that stood on the land before the current buildings. He apparently arose from the grave because he disapproved of the man his daughter planned to marry! Fresh evidence is hard to find and so it is basically impossible to make any conclusions about the authenticity of this particular story.

Devonport

Fore Street

I lived in Devonport for two years while I was studying for a degree at Plymouth University. I always remember on my initial arrival sitting in the Devonport Playhouse in Fore Street for a briefing and being told that even the police went around in pairs in Devonport due to their fear. We were further informed that we should never go out alone. As far as I know this was meant in terms of the fear of the living rather than the dead! However Fore Street was once the site of a very famous ghost sighting.

In 1808 a man was walking along Fore Street, which was drastically different then to how it appears today, when he spotted Lt Fletcher Christian waking ahead. He called out and ran after him but by the time he caught up with the man, Christian had vanished. At the time Fletcher Christian was wanted for his major part in the infamous mutiny on the *Bounty*, and had not been seen since he had set Bligh and his followers adrift on the high seas. The man who had spotted Christian in Fore Street was a sailor named Heywood who had been on-board during the mutiny and who later was exonerated of any part in the revolt. Heywood had remained in the Navy – eventually becoming a senior captain – and this was why he had been in Devonport that evening.

To see Christian here seemed unlikely as it had been presumed that Christian and his men had found an island and set up new lives there. Later it was believed that this was Pitcairn and that almost all of the mutineers (including Christian) had died there, murdered by Tahitian men. So Fletcher must surely have died many years before the alleged sighting: it seems that Heywood had seen a ghost of the famous mutineer.

HMS Naval Base

At the end of May 2004 I was very privileged to be part of a team, alongside fellow investigators from the Paranormal Research Organisation (UK), who were invited to take part in a unique two-night investigation here. We were invited along by Goldy, a researcher from another team, because of our reputation for using scientific methods and to contrast with this more 'psychically' centred team. It was a unique opportunity to study parts of a working military base looking for signs of paranormal activity. The other team were a group who worked under the leadership of Goldy. They were made up of individuals who all worked under the same collective viewpoint, based on psychic and mediumistic approaches. Their team operated with very different perspectives to our approach and worked independently to us. The benefits of this were that there would be no cross-contamination of evidence between the two teams, making it interesting to see how the results compared.

The investigation led to worldwide media and web attention and it seemed the planet was abuzz with the investigation at Devonport. Websites all over the world were discussing it and debating all possible aspects. It was absolutely staggering how so much attention was given to a small group of ordinary guys, with a bit of knowledge about the paranormal, popping in for a couple of days to visit the Navy!

Previous Activity
There had apparently been quite widespread activity for many years in several prominent areas. One of the areas we were to study was the Master Ropemaker's House – said by some to be 'the most haunted building in Plymouth'. We were also to study the notorious Hangman's Cell. I also collected the following research details (summarised), which the rest of the team were not permitted to see until after the investigation, to make sure they were not at all influenced by the information:

The Master Ropemaker's House
This is a fascinating building dating from the eighteenth century and one that has stood empty for the last few years. There are plans for it to become part of the naval museum and visitor's centre in the future. In a book published in 1996 by Nancy Hammonds, titled *Ghosts of Plymouth*, it was written that the Master Ropemaker's House had been the scene for numerous strange events. These included ghostly footsteps, sudden drops in temperature, vacuum cleaners turning themselves off, and the apparition of a bearded man who hummed tunes, known 'as the smiling sailor'. Hardened naval officers had apparently become very unnerved, and cleaners refused to enter what had then been naval offices. A wren, cleaners and even a Lt Cdr had encountered the presence. Also there had supposedly been talk of an exorcism. Lt Cdr Neil Scruton was quoted as saying: 'I am normally sceptical about ghosts but even I have an open mind on this one. There is definitely something going on'. The smiling sailor may have been a man hanged for murder in the eighteenth century and had allegedly been seen in various areas of South Yard.

Also in the book there is talk of 'the Ropemaster's House', which we assume to be the same building (due to the description). This is associated with several peculiar incidents. These include '…noises which have been heard coming from the empty attic and in the same area a young girl, aged about eight to ten has been observed playing with a doll. She either smiles and walks into the next room or simply disappears'. Local history apparently claims that a girl died here on the day her family moved in. Lights have been found on in the middle of the night by security patrols. Also, a lady was apparently pushed very hard whilst in a particular corridor, and a man has been seen looking from the attic window when the place is empty.

My colleague Tony and myself also attended a preliminary visit earlier in the year where we had the privileged opportunity to talk to a family who had lived in this house from 1968 until 1978. They seemed very level-headed and conversant. After this period of habitation it had become a naval office for hydrography and administration. When the family moved in, the house already had a reputation for strange happenings. They told us of many extraordinary

Devonport Naval Base.

occurrences; in the kitchen they had once found all the Formica surfaces torn to shreds and had no explanation for why it had happened. Both of their daughters had been pushed down the stairs between floors one and two, and one had badly grazed her elbow. In one bedroom a bed had moved and a chest of drawers was pushed; a dressing table was also pushed over. Many strange noises had been heard here; apparently on the night of the *Apollo 13* disaster (11 April 1970) some very peculiar noises, akin to loud banging, were heard, with no apparent source. The link may be that the parts for NASA were made at Devonport.

In the attic bedroom, a little girl was seen standing in the corner (aged five or six) as if she was packing a crate. One of the sisters spoke to her on the day they moved in and asked her what she was doing. The girl replied that she was 'moving', and passed her a doll. She took it and then gave it back. The girl was described as having blond hair and playing with a toy box. In the same room a man resembling a sailor has been seen sitting in a wardrobe. In the attic bathroom, a naval officer dressed in an eighteenth-century uniform has been seen. He was often described as staring from the window or looking at people in the bath. Once, the mirror fell with no apparent explanation.

A horse and carriage has been heard outside.

Military police have often reported lights coming on since the building became empty. I read some detailed notes written by the family some time before, which confirmed much of what they told us, but in addition the following had occurred: in the main bedroom, a lady in a creamy/fawn gown with brown velvet trim had been seen, and in recent years, when they paid a return visit and whilst they were in the kitchen, one of the granddaughters burst into tears; she had seen a head on the wall, which suddenly disappeared.

Devonport Naval Base (kindly provided by Will Brunning).

Also a man who served in the Admiralty Police in the dockyard during the 1960s contacted me to say that he had had a very strange experience here. Martin was often on night duty in South Yard, which included the area of the Ropemaster's House. In his own words:

I never did see anything but felt as though I was not alone on many occasions. I was on duty in South Yard entrance one very hot Saturday afternoon; an employee came up to the gate to say that a window had been left open in the Ropery. I 'draw' the keys, goes down to the building, shirt sleeve order, and went up the outside staircase to the third floor, I went a long way up the building before I came to the open window. Something would not let me get near the window; the whole building felt like a fridge, I was driven from that building. The window remained open. As I was on duty 2.00 p.m. to 10.00 p.m., I was later patrolling that part of the yard during the evening. That window was CLOSED. None of the police had been there. Makes you think!

The Hangman's Cell

This was built in 1766 as the tarring and wheelhouse for the nearby Ropery. It is alleged that it was used during the Napoleonic Wars for executing French prisoners of war. The French officers were apparently permitted to carry out their own disciplinary measures and, supposedly, 141 prisoners were executed in this building. They were mostly hanged above a trap door and lowered into a dissection room below (both still present). The Plymouth hangman would attend to oversee proceedings. There was a limepit outside for the bodies. A nail was knocked into the wall each time an execution was over. Crime in the dockyard was rampant and, in the nineteenth century, executions were carried out with a mechanised trap door (now the only one in the country still in working order and used in many films and television productions). In the back wall of the cell is an archway and on the other side is a bricked-up opening. It is said that prisoners were shot through this gap if the rope didn't do its job. There are several headstones of executed prisoners in nearby Stoke Damerel churchyard.

Devonport Naval Base (kindly provided by Will Brunning).

In the 1960s there was an open area next to the Hangman's Cell which was covered with timber. When it rained, lime could be seen bubbling up between the boards. A man is said to have hanged himself here in the last century, and a murder was committed in a nearby latrine.

The base commander informed us that recently members of the military police patrolling the area have heard banging noises coming from the cell when nobody could have been in there. In 1964 a naval rating (Paul) looked into this cell on Christmas Eve (whilst on tour of duty) and told me what he witnessed. In his own words, 'I looked in and there was the trap and a rope gently swinging ...I did feel uncomfortable in the eerie surroundings. I didn't linger, cold and wet, and with a quick thought as to what happened only a hundred years before'.

The Ropery
In this area a man has apparently been seen (source: *Ghosts Of Plymouth* by Nancy Hammonds) wearing a wide belt and braces over an unjacketed shirt.

The Investigation Itself
So much happened that it was almost easy to lose sight of the real reason why we were there in the first place; to carry out an investigation. We spent two full nights at the base, and in fairness it was relatively uneventful; evidence was disappointingly minimal. Just about every member of the team photographed light anomalies, and there were also some stranger photographs picked up as well. These include a 'swirling' blue light (that if you zoom in does take the form of a face – though obviously faces are apparent in lots of images, and are not necessarily paranormal in origin!), and a misty light.

We also captured several moving orbs on nightshot video camera, especially in the Hangman's Cell. There were too many light anomalies to list; some were standard moving ones, while others flashed brightly. We also picked up a strange 'steam effect' in the Ropemaker's House. As we have always stated, most orbs have logical explanations which can be linked very quickly in relation to the camera itself. However, it was most interesting to note that a lot of the orbs appeared at prominent moments; for example, during a séance the orbs appeared at times when we hummed the French national anthem (the spirits there are believed to be those of Napoleonic prisoners of war) and during a time when we spoke a little French. While humming the French anthem and talking in French, light anomalies were caught on night vision. Two members also heard a strange humming sound which they couldn't place and also a flux on the EMF meter was recorded at which point an orb passed the camera! However, no conclusive evidence was obtained.

We also saw a very peculiar 'wispy' shape which flew past the arm of one of the team while he was dowsing.

During a session on the bottom floor of the Hangman's Cell we had camera interference on both the still and moving cameras, including severe battery drainage in a digital camera. At one stage we left a locked-off night-vision camera in an area on the third floor of The Ropemaker's House. This was an area where several people had earlier felt disturbed. On our return we discovered that the lights had been switched on about halfway through the locked-off camcorder session. The light switch for the third floor is on the second floor landing, so we instantly felt that this was very possibly due to human interference, rather than paranormal activity. However, the person leading the group on the second floor insisted that the lights were not touched on their way down, which was confirmed on the tape as he can be heard to open the door and call up to see if anyone was there sometime after the lights had been turned on. We cannot rule out human interference but it was certainly interesting, and the lights had not been turned on by anyone obvious!

In the lower part of the Hangman's Cell base tests were all carried out efficiently and all natural variations were recorded. However, later in the evening a strong EMF fluctuation occurred a metre into the doorway. This disappeared very quickly. Further EMF fluctuations were then obtained on the base of a chair stacked on top of another. This was first picked up on one EMF meter, then to a lesser extent on two others. The reading was still there when the chair was moved. Noting that all three EMF meters are the same make and model, perhaps the small difference in readings indicates that one EMF meter is pre-calibrated to a slightly more sensitive degree.

Another investigator also picked up a strange orange light anomaly on his camera in this room at a time when, unknown to the rest of the team, another had experienced a sensation of pressure building up in her head, which then suddenly went. Nothing was said, to avoid autosuggestion, but immediately afterwards two others also experienced a headache.

One interesting occurrence – which shows how you must always make sure you seek a rational explanation before jumping to conclusions – occurred on the second night. A Naval officer showed us a photo taken the night before in the Ropery, apparently showing a clear figure. It did appear impressive, but we later took a large number of photographs in the (very large) building and eventually managed to recreate it several times. It was nothing more than a pattern on the floor. It is always important to wait for a clear picture before jumping to any supernatural conclusions! If nothing else the whole investigation was an experience never to be forgotten; to be part of a first-of-its-kind investigation at a working naval base. It was a fascinating place and the Navy gave us a very warm welcome and were incredibly hospitable.

We read in the press that the other team were apparently convinced the areas were definitely haunted. In many ways I suppose it was to be expected from a team consisting entirely of mediums, but personally we found nothing scientific or otherwise to conclusively make such a claim. We thoroughly enjoyed our two nights at the base and all felt perfectly comfortable, including in the Hangman's Cell, which the other team apparently found extremely 'hostile'.

In answer to the question 'is the base haunted?' our answer would have to certainly be; 'the jury is still out'!

Above: *A plaque dedicated to the Devon Witches, Exeter.*

Left: *Oak Tree, Exeter (kindly provided by Debbie Lewis – Exeter City Council).*

Exeter

I love the city of Exeter and feel it has the perfect balance between modern and historical areas; it has been populated for at least 2,000 years. A couple of years ago my wife and I were privileged enough to be given our own private ghost walk and personal guide around Devon's capital. We ended up walking around with the fascinating Red Coat for over two hours and hearing all about Exeter's wonderful ghost stories. I am incredibly grateful to Exeter City Council for arranging this (http://www.exeter.gov.uk). Exeter is simply a magnificent city, oozing in history and ghost stories; what more could one ask for? If you've never been – shame on you!

Bedford House

The Spanish wife of Charles I once resided in Bedford House; their daughter Henrietta-Anne was born here. During the Civil War, most of Exeter's town chambers were supporters of the Parliamentary cause, so the Queen left; however, Henrietta-Anne was left here, and imprisoned for two years. The Queen's ghost, accompanied by her faithful servant Hudson, is said to be seen walking down the street and is believed to have come to rescue her daughter, though she may well be four centuries too late!

Bedford Street

This street is certainly a place of change and modernisation but there once stood a Dominican priory here. After the Crusades a knight called Sir Henry lived here and requested that his remains be buried at the priory, in return for giving it much of his wealth. However on his death the cathedral tried to claim his body and bury him instead. Rumour has it that they did this so that they could lay claim to his wealth and so, not surprisingly, a dispute began between the cathedral and priory. Meanwhile poor Sir Henry's body was continually passed between two burial sites.

Eventually it was agreed that the Pope should decide and so, while they waited, Henry was buried in a cathedral chapel site. After two years the Pope finally agreed that the priory should win 'the prize', and so the body was moved yet again. Then, during the dissolution of the monasteries, his lead coffin was dug up and stolen and his bones scattered around. All of this movement seems to have disturbed the knight's soul, as his kindly spirit is now believed to remain here and many people are said to feel his presence, especially in late autumn.

Cathedral of St Peter

The cathedral of Exeter has stood in one form or another for nearly a thousand years and enjoys a tranquillity and spiritual quality that appeals to thousands of visitors every year; people cannot fail to be impressed by this grandiose structure.

A monastery was built here in around 1040 and the third Bishop of Exeter, William Warelwast (nephew of William the Conqueror, who had taken Exeter in 1068) began work on a mighty cathedral to replace the monastery. This began in around 1110 and took almost fifty years to complete. In 1260 the cathedral was then demolished, with the exception of its two Norman towers, and the cathedral, as we know it today, took shape over the subsequent 130 years.

In the cathedral itself a wraithlike nun has made an appearance on certain warm evenings, usually in July. She glides from the south wall of the nave across the cathedral and then, as any classic ghost should, vanishes through a wall. People have often heard chanting, singing and a voice saying 'hello' in the area of St James' Chapel when nobody is present. In St Catherine's Chapel the ghosts of two lovers (perhaps a nun and a monk?) have been witnessed. The ghost of a past caretaker/verger, whose love of the cathedral was legendary, has been witnessed in one of the chapels on a number of occasions. The deanery is also reputedly haunted and, finally, a priest in a cassock has been seen moving between Lady Chapel and the vestry.

In the past a merchant's daughter supposedly committed suicide and her father wanted her to be buried in the cathedral yard. However, being consecrated ground, this was not permitted. Since then it is said that during the first snow of winter a glass-sided hearse will be seen, driven by six black horses and the merchant's ghost, heading across the cathedral lawn. If you look into the merchant's eyes it is terribly bad luck, as a sailor and his girlfriend discovered in the 1940s. They apparently did exactly this and both died soon afterwards.

The lawn in front of the cathedral is said to have been a burial ground for plague victims, however the bodies may have been removed at some time in the past.

Cathedral Close/Yard

The Bishop Bronscombe built parts of Cathedral Close in the late thirteenth century. The Close was the literary point of departure for Jonathan Harker's trip to Transylvania in Bram Stoker's *Dracula*, and a white house here is often called Harker's house. Some claim Mia, one of Dracula's malicious mistresses, now haunts it – a strange claim for a literary character! It is said that Dracula

Exeter Cathedral.

Harker's House,
Cathedral Close, Exeter.

Mol's Coffee House,
Cathedral Close, Exeter.

himself is sometimes seen in the form of a bat; could this not just be a bat? At the timber-framed Mol's Coffee House, Drake is said to have met with people such as Frobisher, Greville, John Hawkins and Sir Walter Raleigh. It is currently the SPCK bookshop and riotous noises are heard at night coming from the empty building.

People wandering around the Close late at night have on occasions seen a hooded figure mooching about looking very much like a monk. Indeed Exeter was a place that had so many monks in times gone by it used to be nicknamed Monktown! This spectral monk is rumoured to be Brother John, who committed the 'heinous' crime of falling in love with a nun. As a result of their guilt they both threw themselves into a well in a building in Cathedral Close and drowned. This same building, now a cafe, used to be the priest's houses, and the back courtyard is said to be where a mortuary was once sited for a period of about sixty years up until the reformation. Since then, many peculiar happenings have occurred in the building, including the aroma of rose water, strange cold draughts and the occasional glimpse of a shadowy figure and the feeling of a presence. Apparently John hates to be ignored, and it is suggested that visitors should say 'hello John' so as not to upset him. In the upper part of the building allegedly resides what is believed to be a poltergeist called Ethel who carries out a variety of mischievous behaviour. Incidentally, the Cowick Barton Inn in Exeter is also believed to be haunted by an ecclesiastical brother.

In other houses in the Close several strange occurrences have happened, including heavy breathing, swishing sounds, doors opening and closing by themselves, footsteps being heard and, in one building here, people have seen an elderly man, without any feet, wearing a nightcap and gown. In yet another building a sailor dressed in late eighteenth-century uniform has been seen reading a newspaper, and outside of a building a lady once saw two medieval soldiers standing outside the archway. Her dog became very agitated and she later discovered that a gatehouse once stood here.

In the Cathedral Yard a lady in black is believed to haunt the surrounding area: she once made a famous appearance when two young men were trying to steal slate from a nearby roof. The ghost appeared and scared them away, saving the valuable tiles.

Catherine Street

This is where the almshouses were situated and at night several people have heard the sound of singing, music and Irish voices here.

Customs House

The sounds of horse's hoof beats clattering on cobblestones have been heard here at this historic quayside building. On one occasion a lady witnessed a cart being led by two horses with a driver sat up top heading into the building. It certainly is an atmospheric construction, and with such a historic past it is perhaps not surprising that paranormal activity has been noticed on more than one occasion.

Guildhall

The Guildhall has been the centre of Exeter's civic life for more than eight centuries and is the oldest such building in the country. A structure of outstanding architectural interest, it remains a busy working place – still in regular use for a variety of civic functions and meetings. Many of the dramatic historical events of Exeter's past have occurred here. In the fifteenth century men were imprisoned here before facing execution the next day on the scaffold outside. Judge Jeffreys presided over sessions of the 'Bloody Assizes' here in 1685, and right up to the early nineteenth century people were sentenced to death or transportation for a wide variety of crimes, which were often very minor offences. People have heard rustling silk and then seen a lady with a piercing stare in the cellars underneath and the next-door shop. She may have been someone

Above left: *Customs House, Exeter.*

Above right: *Turks Head, Exeter.*

relating to the dungeons that were sited here for the purpose of criminal incarceration. Many also report a melancholic atmosphere. However, there is no overall grand tradition of ghostly activity in the Guildhall despite the building's age and grandness. The pub next door – the Turk's Head – was once the frequent of none other than Charles Dickens, and is apparently haunted by a beautiful red-haired young lady.

Marks and Spencer

It is difficult to imagine this store having a ghostly heritage but apparently it does. It is rumoured that it was built on top of a former Roman burial ground, and apparently three skeletons were found in the ground when they built the store. Several strange incidents have occurred here of a poltergeist nature; this has included things being thrown around and strange noises being heard. In the food hall, down in the basement, several previous members of staff have seen a shadowy form drift up and down the aisles and others have felt very uncomfortable, especially by the warehouse door.

Prospect Inn

Positioned on Exeter's quay and originally called 'The Fountain', this 200-year-old pub appeared in the television programme *The Onedin Line*. A 'Christmas' child supposedly haunts the pub. She is described as a little Victorian girl and makes an appearance mainly at Christmas time; she is seen smiling and clutching her little rag dolly before fading away. Other strange occurrences have been reported here at the pub, including strange rapping noises and spinning beer barrels. This may be related to a former landlord who committed suicide and may have subsequently haunted the pub.

Above left: *Prospect Inn, Exeter.*

Above right: *Royal Clarence Hotel, Exeter.*

Royal Clarence Hotel

This was once the town house of the great Sir Walter Raleigh, though to my knowledge no claims have been made that his ghost now haunts the building. On one occasion a man came to visit Raleigh to ask for his help. Apparently he'd had an argument with his friend – a Dutch sea captain. The captain had tried to make up with him but had died before he could do so, and had since been relentlessly haunting his chum. It is claimed that Raleigh blew smoke at the ghost and ever since this spook has haunted the building – often heard coughing, presumably due to the blown smoke!

Also, the Duchess of Clarence lived here, and would often sit in a window watching for the return of her husband, who later became William IV. Some claim her figure is still seen in her familiar place in a window at the front.

St Stephen's Church, High street

This is an amazing little church, which is said to be mainly fifteenth century, though there is an Anglo-Saxon crypt. About ten years ago the authorities proceeded to open this, and when they did, a very strange black mist came out of the slit. So scared were they that they immediately resealed it and left it as it was.

Ship Inn

I adore the Ship Inn which is located in a back street not too far from the cathedral. It has a strong nautical theme and a largely wooden interior with delightful wooden beams and a stone fireplace. Sir Francis Drake reportedly frequented the pub in the late sixteenth century and he and other Elizabethan naval officers such as John Hawkins and Humphrey Gilbert would meet in the pub to discuss battle plans to later be used against the Spanish Armada. In happier times

Ship Inn, Exeter (kindly provided by Kevin Hynes).

they would drink vast amounts of ale and make merry. Drake apparently loved it here, and once wrote: 'next to mine own shippe I do most love that old 'Shippe in Exon'.

It is suggested that Drake and other Elizabethans may still haunt the pub. People have often heard footsteps coming from upstairs when nobody can possibly be up there, and one cleaner was, on two separate occasions, pushed down a short flight of steps.

Drake apparently took the landlord's son on his final voyage and they both died. The ghost of his mother is said to sometimes be seen at night looking out of an upstairs window, a sad expression etched on her face as she grieves for her lost son! I was once here when a lady also visiting the pub was having a drink at a table when she got a strong impression (she makes no claims to be psychic) of an old man by a window, wearing a flat cap. In fact she felt he was a farmer called Tom and simply couldn't shake off the impression.

Southernhay Hospital

This was built in the 1790s as Exeter's first hospital. Back in 1949 a nurse saw a Grey Lady walking in a corridor and asked her colleagues who had been there, only to find out there hadn't been anyone else in the area. It seems to have been a ghost in an old-fashioned uniform. At the top of the building they used to store the skeletons of executed prisoners before they were dissected for medical research. One of these was a Mr Arundel, who had bludgeoned his mother and father to death; his corpse was stored here for over a century. The area is reported to contain a cold and oppressive atmosphere.

On the nearby lawn, between east and west Southernhay, public executions were previously held. Ladies were often burnt at the stake and men hung, drawn and quartered. In 1686 this became a very busy place as Judge Jeffreys sentenced people to death at the 'Bloody Assizes' – either at the Guildhall or Rougemont Castle. Eighty people were sentenced by the black cap and the executioner employed the services of a local butcher to assist him. A quarter of the bodies were then tarred and hung from nearby trees as a deterrent to other Civil War rebels. At night people in the area report a very strange and unpleasant atmosphere.

Incidentally, where the flag of the Rougemont Hotel in Queen Street stands is where the gallows used to be.

South Street

My wife and I stayed a night at The White Hart Hotel a couple of years ago and I specifically asked to stay in a haunted room. My wife was unaware of this in advance but said she had strange feelings about the room – room No.1. I took a photo and an orb was present at the exact spot she focused on. Now I am very sceptical of orbs, which in the main part are undoubtedly explainable quirks of digital cameras and not, as many suggest, spirit energy. However I must admit that it was slightly peculiar that it appeared at exactly the right spot.

The White Hart is one of Exeter's oldest hotels and is located within the old city wall, near to where the south gate stood. It is a fifteenth-century inn, though most of it now actually dates from the 1970s. It is thought it was originally a resting place for monks and later became a coaching inn. Interesting features include the fifteenth-century wine room and an old stone fireplace.

One of the ghosts said to haunt this place is the infamous hanging Judge Jeffreys. In truth his ghoulish perambulations must be exhausting as he allegedly haunts almost as many places as Anne Boleyn. Nevertheless he is certainly known to have held court in Devon and, indeed, in Exeter at the Guildhall. Also here, witnesses have spied a young woman dressed in a long cloak appearing at the front of the building, and a child's face appearing in one of the bar's windows.

At the rear is the courtyard well from which, many years ago, a horrible smell began emanating. A young man was reputedly sent down to investigate and never returned, so another went: the same happened. Apparently the sounds of cries for help have been heard coming from the well ever since. Also nearby is a building with a medieval tower that used to be a debtor's prison. It is here that the expression 'living on a shoestring' arose, and many people report a feeling of sadness permeating the building.

The car park of the Southgate Hotel was formerly a burial ground for the Holy Trinity church, with many a cholera victim buried there. Nearby is the Luddites Tower where people were imprisoned. Witnesses have described seeing the top half of people walking along, and indeed the floor would have previously been at a different level than today!

Tinley's Pizza Express

I have been known to enjoy a pizza and glass of wine in this place, and it is a splendid old building that used to be a tearoom until the 1980s – apparently 'the finest in Devon'. The current building has submerged the original timber-fronted building of the early sixteenth century, which stood adjacent to Broadgate – one of seven gates which kept the cathedral area closed at night! Allegedly Old Friendly Fred, complete with brown sandals, haunts it. Some claim that he is a former gatekeeper/porter who, one night in 1285, failed to close the gate; as a result an intruder entered the cathedral area and murdered a priest or clergyman named Walter Lechlade as he came for morning prayers at 2 a.m. The church petitioned the King for an investigation and as a result the mayor, Alfred Duport, and 'Fred' were both executed for negligence. The only inconsistency is that it was actually South Gate which was left unlocked! Incidentally the murderer was never discovered.

People have also heard strange noises, including tapping and footsteps, reverberating around the restaurant, and laid-up tables are often discovered strewn around, especially on the first floor. A number of people have sensed a young monk here! It may once have been a priest's house, and may be haunted by two problematic priests.

Above left: *White Hart, Exeter.*

Above right: *Tinleys, Exeter.*

Well House Pub

In the cellar here lies the skeleton of either someone who committed suicide or a plague victim. In 2001 an academic from Exeter University claimed that this skeleton was part male and part female, and some claimed it could be parts of Martha and John, the nun and monk who drowned themselves in a well in Cathedral Close. There is also a remarkable Roman well in the cellar and it is this that gives the pub its name. There is often a strange atmosphere in the cellar and a very warm sensation, strange in itself for such a room.

Haytor

Years ago, there were allegedly a number of visions of a 'spectral' cottage within nearby woods on the edge of Dartmoor National Park. The house would appear to certain people at certain times, yet others who were with them would be completely unaware of it. Similarly, some who returned to search for it later were very disappointed not to find it again or any sign that there had ever been a house in the area. The witnesses all reported it independently yet their descriptions were very similar. Most of these sightings occurred in the 1960s. Let's hope this was not in any way related to the widespread use of hallucinogenic drugs!

Rock Inn, Haytor Vale.

Haytor Vale

The Rock Inn

Based on my last visit, this has to be the busiest country pub I have ever seen. I visited on a Saturday afternoon in April and could not believe how many people and cars were present at such a remote inn, nestled beneath the imposing Haytor Rock. It is also interesting to note that clearly none of them had been put off by the ghost story attached to this country-style pub, but were evidently more attracted by the pub's good 'wine and dine' reputation, eye-catching solid stone walls and many little nooks and crannies.

As is consistent with many of the remote pubs of Dartmoor, this was originally founded as a coaching inn in the eighteenth century and the tale attached to the pub is associated with this very coaching heritage. Approximately 200 years ago a serving wench named Belinda began an affair with a coachman who often visited the village. Unfortunately, unbeknown to Belinda, her beloved was already married and when his wife discovered their illicit relationship she was most displeased. The spouse enacted her revenge by murdering Belinda within the confines of the Rock Inn. For the last two centuries Belinda is believed to have remained residing at the hostelry in phantom form, often providing guests with an unexpected encounter. Several people have been victim to her night-time 'poltergeist-like' activities. The main focus for this seems to be centred on the electrics playing up and being turned on when nobody is present. Peculiar noises have been heard in the upstairs part of the building. However, more dramatically, several startled witnesses have also seen Belinda both in the upper part and in the area of the stairs. She is described as wearing a grey uniform and often going about her cleaning duties as if still alive.

Her apparition is apparently so lifelike that when an ex-prime minister stayed here, one of his bodyguards reputedly shot at poor Belinda, leaving a hole in the ceiling.

Ilsington

There is a similar story in Ilsington to the one about a phantom cottage at Haytor. This complete and quaint-looking building has been seen several times in nearby woodland and yet, as soon as people approach the house, it disappears. On closer inspection there are absolutely no building remains at the site where it has been witnessed. Also in the village is a particular old cottage apparently haunted by a local lady. At the beginning of the nineteenth century the lady of the house died, and ever since strange noises have been heard at her former home.

Lewtrenchard

Church / Churchyard

The church has an upside-down cross on the front, and many of the gravestones have odd marks such as skulls and mythical figures. Oddly for the era, many of those buried there are over a hundred years old – a grand feat in the eighteenth century! There have been quite a number of strange reports from within the churchyard and church. For example, there was once a local belief that two phantom white pigs haunted the churchyard. These porkers were described as being joined together by a silver chain. Also see the entry for the manor for other strange goings-on!

Manor Hotel

This Jacobean manor, of which the original house was included in the Domesday Book, is now a luxury hotel set in tranquil parkland on the edge of Dartmoor. In the past it was home to the adventurer James Gould, the gambler and suspected murderer Edward Gould and, from 1872-1924, the folklore writer and famed composer of *Onward Christian Soldiers*, the Revd Sabine-Baring Gould. Regrettably, while his presence has undoubtedly left its mark, not least with his writing desk and portrait situated in the entrance hall, there are no known claims that he haunts the manor.

The ghost that is seen at Lewtrenchard is said to be that of Lady Margaret Baring-Gould, who resided here in the eighteenth century. She was said to be a formidable individual who built up the estate after her husband's death, and she died in her favourite chair in 1795. Allegedly, at the moment of her death her spirit was strong enough to rampage around the room opening windows, and was later seen several times around the grounds. Since her death she has also been seen wandering in the surrounding countryside, especially around Lew Valley, Galford Down and in the nearby churchyard. Her spectre has more recently been seen in what is referred to as the 'Haunted Gallery', and is often described as an elderly lady in old-fashioned costume. Her presence has also been noted in other rooms, including bedrooms. Purportedly her tomb was opened in the churchyard in 1832 and she supposedly sat up, jumped from the vault and chased the poor man who had done so. Allegedly seven local priests were called and turned her spirit into that of an owl, which also now on occasions flies around near the manor house.

Other reported phenomena here include ghostly footsteps, the sound of laughter, and the sound of a carriage moving up the driveway. Revd Baring-Gould and his family also described experiencing several of these phenomena.

When I visited the manor it was the morning of a wedding and a beautiful April day; certainly there was no sign of anything paranormal. In fact, overall it is a very charming hotel. However,

Top right: *Ilsington*.

Above and right: *Lewtrenchard church*.

Below right: *Lewtrenchard Manor*.

I later learnt of another story I had not previously known of referring to a wedding (source: my friend Richard Jones – *Haunted Houses of Britain and Ireland*). In the eighteenth century Susannah Gould got married at Lewtrenchard church, but on her way back to the manor died of a sudden heart attack. Her sad ghost is now sometimes seen on the driveway where the tragedy occurred. Perhaps someone of a more psychic nature than myself might have been attuned to her spirit and able to comment on how she felt about this modern-day wedding?

Above: *Lydford Castle.*

Left: *Lydford Castle (kindly provided by Kevin Hynes).*

Lydford

Castle

This was described in an act of Henry VIII as '… the most annouis, contagious and detestable place in the realm', and it is true that many people were condemned to suffer in this castle. Built in the twelfth century, Lydford Castle was a place of imprisonment and execution. Nevertheless, when I visited here with my wife we both found it to be a thoroughly charming place; the sun was shining brightly, and, apart from a handful of German tourists, there was not another soul around. However, Debbie did get a strange claustrophobic feeling related to an area that we later learnt to have once been the prison dungeons. When the castle was in full operation these cells could only have been reached via a trap door.

An old rhyme states: 'I have often heard of Lydford Law, How in the morn thay hang and draw and sit in judgement after'. The castle was used to issue forth punishments against Devon folk who breached local laws and throughout the Civil War. The bastion is said to hold the ghost of none other than the infamous hanging Judge George Jeffreys. Though his soul is claimed to haunt many a place, the story here is somewhat altered and, dare I say, bizarre, as the judge is said to return in the form of a black pig. However, as there is no documented evidence that he ever visited here, this has to be very debatable.

Another story suggest that Lady Howard also haunts the castle, though she too would appear to be a phantom 'animagus', as she appears in the form of a black dog (synonymous with Devon perhaps?). More recently, the haunting appears to take the form of feelings more than anything. Many people claim to be overcome by feelings of depression and suffering whilst standing within the confines of the fort itself. Others report sudden and involuntary shivers, even on the warmest of days.

Dartmoor Inn

Just before you turn off the main road to head towards Lydford, you pass the Dartmoor Inn. This place is full of character and atmosphere and is a sixteenth-century former coaching inn. This is an inn that seems to back up the idea that ghosts tend to play up when things change in their place of residence; a phantom manifests itself whenever a new landlord/landlady takes over the running of the inn. Much of the goings-on are akin to mischievous poltergeist activity. Indeed it is claimed that on one occasion two glasses were seen floating from the bar by several witnesses before they plummeted and smashed on the floor.

Gorge

Not far from the castle is the entrance to the dramatic ravine known as Lydford Gorge. This has a chequered history and, in the seventeenth century, was the abode of many local thieves. It is also a place where there have been an abundance of suicides over the years. The ghost of an old woman with a red headscarf, sometimes carrying a basket, is believed to haunt Kit's Steps here. Many locals are under the impression that this is a local lady who slipped and fell to her death on her way home from market some years back. She often stands near the pool in shadowy form and some witnesses have claimed to have seen her slip and fall in, but moments later there is no sign of anyone being there.

Lynton

The Lyn and Exmoor Museum

The museum website states: 'A charming, rural museum with a collection of agricultural and domestic tools from Lynton and Exmoor. Housed in Lynton's oldest surviving domestic dwelling, it even includes its own ghost!' Information available would suggest that this might be absolutely right!

In the 1930s this was a cottage called St Vincent's, and one child who stayed there at the time was absolutely petrified by one particular room and refused to sleep there. Then a little boy later slept in the same room and every night at about 9 p.m. would start to scream, claiming to have seen a lady who was 'nasty'. Other people who stayed in the same room at a later date confirmed this, with some refusing to stay the night there. In what used to be the scullery people have heard a sound exactly like a child crying bitterly. Eventually a hidden cupboard was discovered behind a wall and in it was found a bundle of bones, a dead bat and a child's boot – the bones were given to the police. Then, for a while, the house grew quiet, until another incident occurred a few months later when the owner of the house came face to face with a spectral old lady. She was wearing an old-fashioned sage-green dress with a wide bonnet.

Other things that were experienced included footsteps, both inside and outside, feelings of an unseen presence and being followed around the house. Eventually it transpired that the cottage had previously been used as a house to look after young children whose parents were unable to take charge of them. One of the children disappeared, and was never found! The ghost seen by the owner was believed to be the child's mother – perhaps thankful that the child had finally been discovered?

Above left: *Dartmoor Inn, Lydford.*

Above right: *Lynton Museum.*

Olde Coache House

This is an interesting building; now used as a cafe, it is to be found in the main street. You can find it as you head towards the church, after coming down the steep hill into the town. The building was built in the mid-eighteenth century and has had many differing purposes over the years, including that of an apothecary. It has also generally been referred to as a haunted property where strange things have been known to occur amongst the cream teas! For starters, a friendly old man in a long coat and hat supposedly haunts the building. This is believed be a certain Mr Davey who used to work here as a pharmacist at the beginning of the twentieth century. He has appeared on numerous occasions, usually wearing a broad and cheerful grin. It is believed he is a helpful spirit, especially when it comes to anyone suffering from ill health.

Valley of the Rocks

This area was reportedly the roaming ground for a werewolf – sightings were allegedly reported up until the 1990s!

Lynton Church

Lynton church is situated in the centre of the village, with tombstones rising well above the level of the road. There is a traditional story (similar to those in other villages) that the intention was to build it on the Barnstaple road, but while the workmen brought materials or worked by day, the pixies carried the stones away by night. Eventually the builders grew tired of their unproductive labour and constructed it on the spot apparently chosen by the fairy folk.

Ragged Jack Tor

Not far from Lynton in the north-Devon countryside lies a great, rugged, and tremendously jagged tor. There is a legend attached to this area that some Druids were dancing here on a Sunday and carrying on in high revelry when Satan himself suddenly appeared in the midst of them and turned them into stone. The tors standing here today are therefore said to be Ragged Jack and his carousing associates.

Bridge Ball

At nearby Bridge Ball there is a classic black dog appearance, as is so often the case in and around Devon. An animal the size of a black Labrador is said to haunt a particular four-centuries-old cottage and the surrounding area. The canine has been seen and heard and people have also felt 'as if touched' by a dog as well. Apparently a similar dog was drowned in the adjoining river some years before.

Martinhoe/Woody Bay

Coastal Path

A friend of mine who lives in this area reliably informed me that the coast path between Martinhoe and Woody Bay is, so it is rumoured, frequented by a stout ethereal monk. This is an idea also described by Peter Underwood in his book *Ghosts of North Devon*. The friar is described as wearing black robes (Benedictine?) and a cowled hood and is often witnessed either following people or standing stock-still nearby. He is said to be short but portly. If anyone is brave enough to approach, the phantom simply vanishes, though not always immediately. Other people have reported that their dogs have behaved strangely in the same area, and that it is often particularly cold and atmospheric here!

Above left: *Martinhoe.*

Above right: *Woody Bay.*

A Benedictine priory was established at Pilton (near Barnstaple) and the monks would have travelled on cart tracks throughout the area. Perhaps this may provide a suitable explanation for such a monk in this district. When I visited this path it was a bright sunny late morning and even with nobody else around it was hard to imagine the place to be at all sinister. However, experience tells me that you often just need to be in the right place at the right time and all that can change in an instant.

Also in Martinhoe there is said to be the indistinct ghostly figure of an old lady adorned in grey.

There is also a bizarre legend relating to Woody Bay about a particular squire who lived nearby. He was reportedly a great gambler and was often penniless as a result; on one occasion when he was nearly cleaned out he resorted to burglary. It was nearly rent day and he knew that the tenant of one of his farms would have the rent money prepared. He decided to break into the farmhouse and steal the cash, knowing that the farmer would still be obliged to pay his rent. He clothed himself in scruffy clothes, took a pair of pistols, and headed to the farm. Here he tried to break open a window but made such a din that the farmer heard him, and shot him dead with a blunderbuss as he was halfway into the house. After this the ghost of the squire apparently haunted the farm. Eventually the local ghost-layer came to carry out an exorcism, but to no avail, and so six parsons were called upon and the spirit was then successfully banished to the top of High Veer Point; his howls of rage are heard in the vicinity to this day.

Moretonhampstead

In June 2004 a team of paranormal investigators visited a shop in the beautiful Dartmoor village of Moretonhampstead, with some fascinating results; the medium that visited with them impressed the whole team despite their apparent scepticism, picking up on things he almost certainly could not have guessed at. A Victorian ornamental door stop, shaped like a cat and covered in dust and cobwebs, was moved in front of a door when nobody was in the area, and nobody seemed to be able to work out where it had come from. Also, a radio suddenly turned on by itself. In the past the owners had reported all sorts of strange activity including things being moved around when they have returned in the morning.

Newton Abbott

I was reliably informed by a lady who used to drive lorries for a delivery company of a story about the company's depot on the Heathfield Industrial Estate. She would sometimes witness strange things here, including objects moving. This would range from keys to a big blue heavy oil drum in the yard. Sometimes she would be changing boxes on the lorry when she would walk around the truck and find the locks had been turned behind her. Sometimes her mobile phone would reveal the message 'how are you', but with no sender; apparently, her colleagues had similar experiences.

One night the unseen presences seemed to surround her and close in as if leading her to the back of the lorry. She was convinced there were three men trying to tell her something. Concerned and a little reluctant, she turned a torch on and lit up the back of the lorry. To her surprise she found that the arm-lock was broken, leaving the door insecure and unsafe. Inside she discovered that several large electrical items were untied and she immediately thought of the mayhem that fridges and cookers could have caused falling out on the motorway. 'That night they saved my butt,' she said. She experienced these unseen men several other times, and it was as if they liked to sneak up when least expected. While she never saw anyone she did feel their presence and sometimes got images in her head of how they may have looked.

She feels that there may well have been a link to Fairfax's New Model Army and their successes in the area in 1646 and that a small battle may have occurred at the site.

Otterton

Ladram Bay

T.C. Lethbridge was a very influential and foresighted man. He had many theories about the paranormal, and was particularly well known for his ideas about water and magnetic fields being possibly responsible for 'playing back' images and feelings, often perceived as ghosts. He quoted an experience he had at Ladram Bay where he was overcome by a 'blanket of depression' whilst walking on the cliffs here, something he referred to as a 'Ghoul'! The account is widely described in other publications but my fellow researcher Stuart Andrews had his own experiences at Ladram Bay. He was visiting with a group one January afternoon (just like Lethbridge himself) and headed to the raised area on the beach described by Lethbridge. He instantly felt feelings of dizziness and 'butterflies' in his stomach, and he seemed to be able to 'walk in and out of it', as though there was an invisible energy. Others in the party seemed able to feel the same sensations at the same place, though not everybody. Stuart admits himself that '...obviously this is not any conclusive evidence of any paranormal activity and many may say that from reading what one was supposed to feel, that the mind made it appear so'. However, the others who did feel this were not familiar with Lethbridge's account. Stuart has also returned on a number of occasions and been totally unable to repeat the experiences.

Ladram Bay (kindly provided by Stuart Andrews).

Fox 'n' Goose Hotel, Parracombe.

Parracombe

Fox 'n' Goose Hotel

Lying on the edge of the River Heddon this pub cannot be missed, lying on the left as you enter the village. It is a perfectly charming and typical Exmoor inn, though no longer offering accommodation but still a warm welcome. It provides good food and service and was recommended by television chef Rick Stein when it appeared on his programme in 2005.

In the past the building has been decimated by fire and flood but survives today as a perfect example of Devon hospitality!

In 1961 the owners of this hostelry described many strange occurrences, including a sense of cold apprehension and feelings of fear in the attic rooms. These feelings developed into more substantial occurrences and on one occasion the bedclothes were ripped away from the lady sleeping in that bed, with absolutely no explanation. Later a black pigeon was found in the same room and seemed to be a prelude to misfortune. This included poor health, a marriage break up and general bad luck. They finally left in 1967 and life took a turn for the better.

Apparently, a girl who had lived in the pub previously had died in the room from ill health. In the 1910s the seventy-five-year-old popular landlord of the hotel, Mr H.R. Blackmore, who had rebuilt the place, had a serious accident on the road to Lynton when his horse kicked him in the leg with such force that his limb eventually had to be amputated. However, he continued to get around with great success with the help of an artificial limb before dying in 1922 due to complications after a chill. Could either of these historical figures be responsible for later phenomena?

ABC Cinema.

Plymouth

ABC Cinema

This former theatre has experienced a wide array of ghostly goings-on in recent times and has therefore gained quite a bit of press attention. Strangely enough, most of the occurrences seem to happen during times when horror films are being shown, particularly in screen two, the most active night apparently occurring during the showing of the film *The Ring Two*! The suspected ghost is that of an actress nicknamed Emily, who may have committed suicide in an old former dressing room. She is described as wearing a long red skirt and jacket with black braiding round the neck and arm areas. On a few occasions people have described seeing a woman sitting in one of the front row seats but when the lights come up at the end of the film, she has vanished. Other goings-on have included drops in temperature, unexplainable noises, seats that look as if someone is sitting in them when nobody is and doors that seem to unlock themselves. One member of staff was so scared he left his job.

In May 2006 a team from the Paranormal Research Organisation (www.paranormalresearch. org.uk) carried out an investigation, and below is a summary, kindly written by PRO's Devon co-ordinator, Kevin Hynes:

> The ABC Cinema, built prior to the Second World War, survived the Plymouth Blitz. This was an exclusive opportunity for the PRO team to carry out an all night investigation at a unique venue.

Sixteen members split into three separate teams to investigate four different areas. The following is a short summary of what was picked up by all three teams in the four areas, which were screen one, screen two, screen three and the rest rooms/stairs:

Screen one – All three teams reported high EMF readings in this area. Also all three teams carried out darkness vigils with some very interesting results. Light anomalies and noises were also picked up.

Screen two – More than one team picked up on the same presence in this screen, that of a young girl who had also been previously picked up by another paranormal group who carried out an investigation some months previously. To the ABC staff's amazement, the presence was picked up in exactly the same area/seat number; coincidence? Light anomalies were photographed and noises were heard coming from the back of the room. Cold spots were felt and one investigator stated that she had been touched by something.

Screen three – Once again all three teams picked up on a lot of similar information and activity. Very interesting results, especially with the EMF meter, whilst one team conducted a darkness vigil and asked for communication: the presence, which had been previously picked up through dowsing, was asked to walk back and forth towards the EMF meter. To the team's amazement, the meter began to fluctuate, giving the impression the presence was trying to converse with us. One of the staff members (a sceptic) had his leg tapped twice, and we were unable to find an explanation.

Rest rooms/stairs – All three dowsers picked up on a number of different presences within these areas which indicated that the presences were moving around the whole building, maybe even following each individual team. Various light anomalies were photographed and captured on night vision. One female member captured what could only be described as a black orb which needs to be analysed for clarification.

Conclusion - A very interesting investigation with some fascinating results and information gathered. Thank you to the manager and the staff for their warm welcome and hospitality. Hopefully we will be able to make a return visit to the ABC Cinema.

Derry's Cross

At the former TSW/Westward television studios, believed to have been built over a former Napoleonic French prisoners of war graveyard, many people had apparently heard loud and sinister laughter accompanied by an extreme drop in temperature and voices speaking in French had been heard.

Devil's Point

It is claimed that here Sir Francis Drake and a set of sorcerers conjured up storms which would later fraught the Spanish Armada. It is now claimed that Drake and the magicians haunt the area uttering their incantations.

Above left: *Sir Francis Drake.*

Above right: *Elizabethan house.*

Elizabethan House

This is a genuine Tudor sea captain's house, sited on Plymouth's historic cobbled Barbican. It contains period furniture, a spiral staircase set around a ship's mast and original wooden beams and windows. Built in the late sixteenth century, it is now owned by Plymouth Council and maintained by the National Trust. In the 1980s a group of visitors heard a strange creaking noise and on investigation discovered a cradle rocking itself; several people witnessed this and the same phenomenon was experienced happening more than once. Other things have happened here, but more than anything it is worth a visit just for the glorious nature of the house.

Grand Hotel

At the time of writing this building is going through extensive renovation work after a massive fire tragically happened here in September 2003. The hotel on Plymouth Hoe suffered extensive damage when an electrical fault caused a major blaze, which ripped through the roof and top two floors. Over a hundred fire fighters and seventeen fire engines were involved in battling the blaze and evacuating staff and guests. The Grand Hotel was one of Plymouth's oldest hotels, and often described as 'Plymouth's flagship'.

It may well be that this disaster had disturbed the resident ghosts, as activity appears to have increased, as noted by more than one workman. In the past staff and guests alike have seen a Victorian lady walking down a corridor. She was apparently a lady whom two men fought over when alive; during their tussle, they accidentally knocked her over the staircase and she fell to her death.

Left: *Grand Hotel.*

Opposite*: Palace Theatre.*

At present the new owner has applied to turn the hotel intwenty-six apartments retaining all the original walls and features – including the whole of the site's restaurant and the original Victorian architectural details typical of the period. However, the costs involved (said to be thirteen million pounds) mean it is very unlikely to be a hotel again. One wonders if activity will continue when the building eventually reopens with a new use!

Railway

In February 1977 a railway worker was travelling on a train heading from Plymouth when the express stopped at engineering works. As a railwayman he had a natural interest in trains and so looked to see what the locomotive at the head of the engineer's train was and clearly read that it was 'D1067 – *Western Druid*'. Not an exciting story maybe, except that the *Western Druid* had been withdrawn from service on the 24 January 1976 and sent to Swindon where it had been scrapped on 9 February 1976! The train had clocked in an impressive 1,232,000 miles during its thirteen years of service; was it perhaps still clocking them up after its demise?

Stoke

In November 2005, PRO (Paranormal Research Organisation) were given the opportunity to investigate a private house in the Stoke area of Plymouth. The tenants had been so scared by events that they had moved out and so we sent in our Plymouth team to investigate!

During this investigation one of the strangest things that happened was that whilst several people were talking in the front bedroom, a piece of wood, which had been leaning against a wall, suddenly moved and fell onto the floor. The team reported that there seemed to be no obvious reason why this should suddenly happen at that moment!

Whilst taking photographs, one team member's cameras batteries drained almost immediately. He insisted that these were brand new batteries, which had been fitted within the hour, and on a few occasions people felt tingling sensations travel up their back. There seemed to be what could only be described as a cold breeze moving around the team. They checked for draughts but were unable to locate any.

They subsequently carried out a group darkness vigil and some investigators did get the impression that something was trying to make itself known. One member felt as if they had had cold hands placed on them and felt tingling around their lower back. Also, very interestingly, at one stage a high EMF reading was recorded near the bed when there had been no obvious reason for this, especially as the EMF reading near the electric socket on the other side of the room had shown less than two. A female presence was apparently standing near the bedhead where the high EMF was picked up. (It is worth noting that the baseline tests had been conducted before the dowser had entered the room and so he didn't know about the high EMF reading in the corner of the room before dowsing).

Overall, everyone was impressed at how much information was picked up; it was certainly a fascinating place. I also later learnt that there is said to be a plague burial ground in the area nearby.

Stonehouse Hospital

In 1950 a male nurse was working at the Royal Naval Hospital one night when he suddenly heard the sound of footsteps. It was like somebody was wearing rubber plimsolls, as the sound was like something squeaking on the polished floor. This was peculiar and he went to investigate with a torch but could not find anyone out of bed or present in the ward, and all the doors were closed. Nevertheless, the footsteps continued, and it was almost as if they were pacing up and down the ward. Apparently this has happened since and indeed before this a few times over the years and to different people. The presence is believed to be that of a naval rating who had been admitted here during the Second World War. He had serious injuries as a result of a bombing raid on Plymouth and was apparently in such distress he managed to throw himself out of the window.

Union Street - Palace Theatre

At the time of writing this Grade II Listed building was being used as a nightclub, the notorious Dance Academy, which is often in the local news, usually with negative storylines. However, in finer times this was the Palace (and New Palace) Theatre, one of the finest Victorian buildings in the town. One of the previous owners was a Mrs Hoyle and her ghost is said to still haunt the building today. I remember in my student days a friend of mine working here as a glass collector and saying it was a very spooky place; he often felt very unnerved, even when it was full of people. The 'ghost' is indeed more frequently felt than seen. Some have claimed that this may be 'Mary', who died in a fire which took several lives in the late nineteenth century. However my research suggests that the only victims of the fire, which happened in 1898, seem to have been a pig and several hens!

Opposite: *Palace Theatre.*

Right: *Boringdon Hall (kindly provided by Kevin Hynes).*

During the Blitz, much of Plymouth was tragically destroyed. After one particular bomb dropped on Union Street two children claimed to have witnessed a lady dressed in white walking in the ruins before vanishing.

Plympton

Boringdon Hall

Situated five miles from Plymouth city centre, this Grade I Listed Elizabethan manor house has been restored to its former glory and retains a definite air of tranquillity and grace. It stood in 1066 and was mentioned in the Domesday Book. In fact, it is probably one of the oldest sites in the area. Until the dissolution of the monasteries it belonged to the local priory of St Peter and was then renovated in the sixteenth century by the Grey, Mayhew and then Parker families. It has previously hosted visits by Elizabeth I, Sir Francis Drake, Sir Walter Raleigh, and many other noteworthy individuals. During the Civil War the owners were Royalists and an attack by Parliamentarian forces destroyed part of the hall. From the eighteenth century it was used as a farmhouse, and in more recent times has been owned by the National Trust and become a grand hotel.

Activity has been widespread in the past and has included a wide range of experiences. Lady Jane Grey – the famed and tragic nine-day Queen – has been allegedly seen both inside and outside the building. Her forlorn and sad figure is seen in Tudor costume and appears to be repeating her actions from the past. Also, the famed mariner Sir Francis Drake apparently haunts Boringdon, as he does so many other locations, here mostly being sighted in the great hall. However, as he only visited on a number of occasions it is not evident as to why his ghost should appear here. The ghost of John Parker, who renovated the building in the sixteenth century, and held parties which the local dignitaries (including Drake) attended, has also been seen.

Strange noises have been heard in various bedrooms; these have included footsteps and banging. Icy temperatures have also been felt here. Other feelings in these rooms include numbness, hot flushes, draughts and a sensation that a man is sitting on the bed. Dark shadows have also regularly been witnessed moving around in the same rooms. One of these rooms is a place where, it is rumoured, a man hanged himself during the Civil War.

A horse and carriage has been heard in the grounds and a lady and her child who died in a fire (or perhaps, jumped from the window) are also believed to haunt the property. Quite a place! Many thanks to Debbie Moss, Operations Manager, for assisting with providing the following written information (www.boringdonhall.co.uk):

It was around the year 956AD that King Edgar granted the manor of Boringdon and Wembury to St Peter of Plympton, so naturally Boringdon Manor belonged to the priory until the dissolution of the monasteries in 1539 by Henry VIII.

Boringdon Hall appears that it might be haunted … if you firmly believe in the paranormal then please read on, and experience our ghost tour.

Upon walking through the grand archway into the hotel, to greet you is a sixteenth-century armour-plated statue. With its realistic stance and posture, it won't come as a surprise that many strange happenings are connected with the armour-plated figure. One particular evening a Night Porter was in training with a newly appointed replacement Porter. They happened to be walking by the figure; as usual the helmet was in the upright position. This was put right, with it in the downward position; both Porters were witnesses to this happening. Exactly two hours into the evening, which seemed calm for that time of night, the helmet was back to its original position, without anyone being around.

The exact same night the trainee Porter, who knew nothing about the hotel's history of spiritual happenings, was walking around the building, in the area looking into the Restaurant Staircase. The shadow he saw moving in a spiral motion towards the top area of the staircase looked almost human. As he knew nothing about the reported shadows, he thought it was a customer or the Night Porter. When getting back together, he explained the situation; both possible explanations were ruled out, as it was early in the morning and the Night Porter happened to be in the Reception area at the said time it was seen.

With the land being in ownership for around 900 years Boringdon Hall Hotel has had a lot of noble men and women pass through its doors. With it being a newly reformed hotel, it appears that some of its past visitors are still around and feeling very unsettled.

Room Fifteen
Everyone who knows this building would be familiar with the stories that surround the four-poster room. Many a guest has spent a night in there, but has never felt settled with the atmosphere around the window overlooking the Wembury grounds. This could be due to the fact that in the seventeenth century, a woman as young as seventeen fell pregnant with the Lord's son's illegitimate child. The idea of this child being brought into a respected family was unheard of at this time. Therefore to spare the child from torment she fell to her death with

the child in her arms. The name of the girl was Isabella. The ghost of mother and child are said to walk the grounds outside room fifteen.

A popular airline company have booked this room; events have occurred in which a gentlemen has felt something or someone sitting on his chest, making it hard to breath. A pass in a plastic wallet has been placed on the bedside cabinet; when he awoke, the card was found ten feet across the room, with the plastic wallet in the same position as it was left.

Room Sixteen
Located on the third floor of the Main House, room sixteen is often the room which feels comfortable, but still unexplainable moments within the room occur. One particular night, a female guest had checked into this room. Deep in sleep she felt nothing untoward. When she finally awoke, the room looked strange compared to how she had left it. Her whole body had been turned around, with her feet near the headboard and her head near the foot of the bed. The unexplainable part of this is that the woman was still tucked in bed, eradicating any possible chance that she could have been involved.

In the Elizabethan Suite people have experienced children playing.

In the Great Hall Bar a tequila bottle once flew off the shelf onto the floor. Three members of staff were present.

Activity has been witnessed in various parts of the hall; key sightings claim to be Lady Jane Grey and Sir Francis Drake. People sleeping in rooms fifteen, sixteen and seventeen have experienced the feeling of someone sitting on the bed and unexplained noises. Staff and residents have seen strange lights and flashes; one visitor is said to have almost fainted in fear of what lay behind the door into room fifteen! Another guest sleeping in room sixteen woke to see a dark shadow crossing the room. Night Porters have also heard loud footsteps and felt cold spots. Sometimes the electricity will cut out for no apparent reason leaving them alone in the dark!

Plymstock

If you are looking for a ghost in Plymstock, street signs might just give you a helping hand. One aptly named street is called White Lady Road and was actually named after the apparent sightings of a resident ghost. The spook has been witnessed in and near the area close to Radford Lake. Some people have claimed to see her crossing the road, whereas others claim she is seen rowing a boat across the lake itself. As a result many residents have for years avoided the area at night.

She is assumed to be the spectre of a lady named Kathleen. The story goes that she was the lover of St Keverne – the Celtic saint. After an argument between the couple he is said to have killed her by beating her to death (nice saint!) or by throwing her into the lake where she drowned.

Postbridge

The East Dart Hotel

A drunken dog allegedly haunts the East Dart Hotel! A former landlady one day was possessed by a sudden religious and salubrious zeal and decided to remove all alcohol from the pub, proceeding to pour it into a nearby ditch. The hound came along and began to lap it up until it fell into a drunken stupor and began howling at the moon. This canine wraith is said to continue to repeat this uncanny manifestation to this very day. Imagine that … getting drunk for all eternity!

B3212

The Hairy Hands is not a story that I can add to with any great effect as it is a story that has been effectively 'done to death'. A series of strange events have occurred along this road giving it the reputation as one of the most well-attested ghost stories in the country. The incidents have included cars veering off the road out of control, occasionally with fatal consequences. Cyclists and motorbike riders claim to have had their handlebars wrenched away by unseen hands, and a number of these witnesses claim to have spotted a pair of vast hairy hands gripping their steering wheel. It is undoubtedly an atmospheric stretch of road, giving one a sense of remoteness and isolation when driving there alone, and it was part of an ancient trackway. I will admit to a level of scepticism relating to the idea of hirsute appendages devilishly grasping at one's steering wheel.

Nevertheless I can state that I was once driving along this road with my wife when our car started to struggle. It was a car that had given us no such problems before the journey or afterwards. However, for a period of five minutes I continually had to drop down the gears on even the slightest incline, as the engine seemed unable to get enough revs. It could well have been a mechanical coincidence, but it was strange that it happened on such a notorious stretch of road. In 2004 I was employed by Vauxhall Corsa to prepare a list of the top ten 'most haunted roads in the UK' for an advertising campaign, and placed the B3212 at the top of the list.

Regrettably, although the story was a personal favourite, they said they could not use such a story relating to traffic accidents, as it would not be good publicity for a car advert. Nevertheless I would maintain that this road must surely be classed as one of the most allegedly haunted roads in the country based on the sheer wealth of independent incidents that have been described here – whether genuine or not.

Princetown

Fogginter Quarry

My friends and fellow paranormal researchers Stuart and Becky Andrews visited a place called Fogginter Quarry, which is situated a few miles from North Hessary, just outside of Princetown. They had not previously visited this place, nor had they heard anything connected with it. It had snowed heavily the previous evening, and continued to shower intermittently during the day. Indeed there was a mist so typical of the moor for the entire day, with it being somewhat overcast.

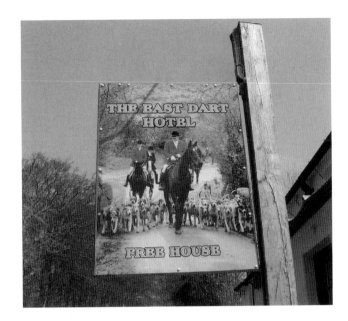

East Dart Hotel, Postbridge.

*Hairy Hands (kindly provided by
Kevin Hynes).*

*Foggintor (kindly provided by Stuart
Andrews).*

However, this had not dampened their enthusiasm to enjoy the day and the sights they would see. As the two of them were walking down through the disused quarry, they were singing and joking. Suddenly, as if walking into an atmosphere of some sort, Stuart's mood changed inexplicably; he began to feel uneasy and aggravated. These feelings came from nowhere, and grew stronger as they neared the bottom of the quarry. Upon reaching the bottom (half of which is covered by a pool of still water), they became more and more uneasy, as if something was watching the two of them. There were no people visible anywhere on the moor for miles. After five minutes or so Becky stated that she wanted to go immediately. Knowing that she is not easily unnerved, and feeling the same, Stuart agreed straight away. As they were making their way through the quarry, around the pool of water to the opposite side, the feelings of insecurity heightened again as they sped away. Such was the unease felt by Becky that she nearly refused to wait whilst Stuart took a couple of photographs.

During the entire time they had been inside the quarry, Stuart had constantly remarked on his feelings, whilst Becky refused to comment. However once they had left the vicinity, she explained in a distraught voice that she had never ever felt something so terrible, or been so glad to leave a place behind her. When they relayed this story to Becky's father, he remarked that he too had felt uneasy on a previous visit to Foggintor Quarry, stating: 'Something very wrong has happened there'. He is a very strong character, who has frequently walked across Dartmoor and other lonely places, both with groups and on his own. Not the sort of man to be influenced by horror stories or fireside tales. Such is his 'no-nonsense' personality he had not mentioned his feelings to Becky or Stuart before they spoke to him of their experience, nor had Becky talked to him about the incident prior to their conversation on the matter.

My research reveals that this is a place where the Army carry out armed commando training. Also nearby is Yellowmeade Cairn, an ancient hut settlement. The granite from the quarry, now dominated by ruins, was used in the construction of Dartmoor Prison and it may be assumed that prisoners would have worked at the quarry as they certainly did aid in the construction of the prison. Goodness knows how many tens of thousands of tons of granite have been extracted from the quarry over the years. One can only wonder what might have happened in this area in the past! (Thanks to Stuart and Becky for kindly providing this account.)

Plume of Feathers Pub

This is the oldest building in Princetown. Built in 1785, it is a traditional family-run inn with copper bars, log fires, oil lamps and plenty of atmosphere, and also retains many of its original features, including slate floors, exposed beams and granite walls. Naturally it is also claimed to be haunted!

The main phenomenon occurs in a room upstairs. Several people staying for bed and breakfast have reported being woken by somebody trying to pull the sheets from their bed. Other strange things occur, including a strange weeping sound and the echo of pacing footsteps, believed to be a poor woman whose child died in the past.

On one occasion startled witnesses saw a lady in a brown cloak who then simply disappeared, though it is not known who she might have been. Another peculiar story relates to the ladies' toilet, where many visitors have felt a frosty draught, although as Princetown is the highest town in the country and seemingly cold even in summer, one cannot I guess discount a natural breeze.

Plume of Feathers, Princetown.

Prince of Wales, Princetown.

Dartmoor Prison, Princetown.

Prince of Wales Public House

This pub, the home of Princetown Brewery, is a welcoming tavern with two open fires – and therefore essential for Dartmoor's infamous windy nights. It also has an array of fascinating old photographs of Princetown and it is believed that it is actually haunted by, of all things, a priest! The pastor has previously been seen drifting across the pub, though nobody seems to know why he would be haunting a tavern but one wag suggested he might be after the Holy Spirit! A former guest some years ago was apparently awoken by a non-existent alarm clock on three following nights at exactly 3.30 a.m., though no reason could be ascertained. Each time she experienced something strange, including seeing a floating white triangle and hearing music.

Prison

Princetown is so called in honour of the Prince of Wales, later George IV, because the whole of Dartmoor forms part of the estates of the Duchy of Cornwall. The notorious prison was originally built in 1806 to house the large numbers of French prisoners of war captured during the Napoleonic campaigns, and was later used in 1812 to imprison captured Americans.

The present prison encompasses an area of about thirty acres and includes the buildings formerly used to house prisoners of war. The old war prison was then acquired in 1850 for incarcerating convicts and it has retained this use ever since. The graveyard is said to be a place for frequent ghostly sightings, assumed to be the phantoms of former prisoners of war.

However, the most famous Dartmoor Prison ghost has to be the shepherd David Davies. He was a man convicted in 1879 for stealing two shillings in Shrewsbury and sentenced to a long period of penal servitude (believed to originally have been thirteen years) at Dartmoor. He stayed at the prison for a very long time – for what some claimed was eventually a total of fifty years. While there he looked after the animals, especially the sheep, and was completely trusted to oversee them on nearby Dartmoor. In 1910 the then Home Secretary, a certain Winston Churchill, looked into his case and, because of Davies' impeccable behaviour, Churchill recommended his release.

Apparently Davies loved his job so much that when released from prison he committed a crime and was back within weeks. He continued to do this for many years until his death in 1929. These crimes included stealing from a poor box in Matlock church in 1918 the sum of eighteen shillings and tenpence (Davies was by now aged seventy-seven!); he was very frustrated to find himself put on remand instead of being returned to Dartmoor.

His unmistakeable ghost, complete with a flock of sheep, has often been seen in the surrounding area of Dartmoor on the mist-swept moor land as if he is still carrying out the job he loved so very much. As you leave Princetown and the prison one cannot help but think about the police notices, 'do not stop your car'.

Shebbear

Devil's Stone Inn

According to their website: 'this is a seventeenth-century former farmhouse and coaching inn. Sitting on the edge of the village square, the pub is a beamed, flagstone-floored building with several open fireplaces'. As you enter the public house there is an imposing wooden staircase that greets you, and the bar is to the right with a restaurant to the left. The inn is also reputedly attached to the church by a hidden tunnel. Supposedly a young girl (aged about seven) wearing a white smock is traditionally said to haunt this pub in north Devon, possibly as a result of a man being murdered here in the past. This youngster is also blamed for apparent poltergeist activity. This has included pictures falling from walls, beds being ruffled, lights being turned on and light bulbs blowing, windows being opened and beer taps being turned on.

The man was said to have been a fugitive who arrived with his daughter; he was later found dead, with little explanation. Some also claim that his ghost, complete with grey beard, has also been seen here in the pub. Lots of people have heard loud footsteps coming from upstairs when in fact nobody is there. Teacher's Whisky once named this as one of the twelve most haunted pubs in the country. A resident chef from a few years ago said he was often possessed by an unnatural feeling, like being watched, making him anxious. He spent some time living in room four and was sometimes awoken by the sounds of someone walking heavily up and down the hallway outside. Whoever it was would walk continuously along the length of the hallway but would periodically stop. This could happen for a long phase of time but there was never anyone there when it was investigated.

The village of Shebbear itself is a predominantly farming village set in the midst of Devon countryside and near Holsworthy. The village is known for its tradition of 'Turning the Devil's Boulder'. On 5 November each year a large stone lying in the village is turned, to ensure prosperity and deliverance from evil for the coming year. The stone was apparently dropped by the Devil himself whilst he was carrying it from heaven to hell. The stone is indeed not local to the area. Personally I would find it hard to resist leaving the stone alone one year to see what might happen!

Devil's Stone Inn (kindly provided by Stuart Andrews).

Stuart Andrews spent an interesting night here with a Devon investigation team and here follows his summary of the evening (with kind permission from Stuart):

For the first session, very little was personally experienced, although the medium present picked up on a good deal of information. However myself and one other member of the team did report a sensation of 'smoky eyes' afterwards. Interesting, as the medium had correctly identified that there had previously been a fire in this part of the building.

During the rest break after this session, I did have a very unusual experience in the hall leading to the main entrance. I was taking some photos, which have produced some unusual light anomalies, when I felt a strong draught on my right hand, moving past me. I was unable to recreate this by opening or closing doors and there was nobody else moving around to indicate a natural cause.

In one room approximately ten orbs were caught on camcorder; one is particularly interesting, as it appears to emanate from one of the staff member's hands. It seems unlikely to me that this was caused by a reflection from her jewellery, as the movement does not indicate this and no other similar possible reflections were caught. One room in particular is reported to be one of the most active rooms, and is always inexplicably cold compared to the rest of the building. A steady-cam locked off in here earlier did not provide any interesting footage; however during the session in here two orbs were caught on camcorder, which appear to be moving from the en-suite. This was interesting as both myself and another investigator separately witnessed an orb-like shape in this area.

A séance was then held in the bar area as a finale to the night with the whole team present. During the last ten minutes or so, I began to be affected by persistent back pain (which I do not suffer from), compelling as I was stood on the spot where one of the old locals had fallen off his stool and died. The staff seemed interested in this and asked if my hands were hot, as he was known as a healer. I have to admit that the back pain was accompanied by my hands becoming very hot! A very interesting investigation with some good findings.

Shute

Shute Barton House

This is an attractive, unfortified manor house dating from the Middle Ages, complete with newel staircase, garderobes, a great open fireplace, open-timbered ceilings and panelled rooms. Work began in 1380 and was finally completed in the late sixteenth century, though parts of the building were later knocked down in the eighteenth century. It has battlemented turrets, late Gothic windows and a Tudor gatehouse. Today, although the property is now in the care of the National Trust, it is still the home of the Pole-Carew family.

The classic ghostly figure of a Grey (or White) Lady has been seen walking the grounds and the figure disappears swiftly if anyone approaches. Some have claimed that this may be the ghost of Lady Jane Grey, who visited the property. However it is perhaps more likely to be a member of the Pole-Carew family as Shute Barton's residents were known to be staunch Royalist supporters. The shade may therefore be a Royalist lady who was, according to legend, hanged in the grounds during the Civil War. The story goes that a lynch mob was waiting for her one day and they swiftly hoisted her up to a tree where she quickly died. The area is still referred to as 'The Lady Walk'. Many of the reports (including some very recent ones) have

Shute Barton, Devon (kindly provided by Stuart Andrews).

been spoken of by people with very little prior knowledge about the history of the building or paranormal stories. Furthermore, dogs have an uncanny habit of acting up in this area, with familiar growling and their hackles standing up on the back of their necks. I know of several people who have found the house positively charming and yet the grounds to be mysterious and unnerving.

There are also reports of a phantom white cat that is mistaken for a normal family pet, at least until it walks through something solid. The cat is seen most often in the garden area. Others have described the cat as being see-through.

Sourton

Highwayman Inn

This has to be the most unique pub I have ever visited, a must-see. It is a veritable Aladdin's cave of Gothic artefacts and peculiar maritime furnishings, a delight to the eye. The building was originally built in 1282 and has always been used as an inn, though at times it also had the dual purpose of being used as a farm as well.

It has been claimed to be the south-west's most haunted pub, and certainly a wide array of paranormal activity has been claimed. This has included the widespread capture of light anomalies and orbs on camera and the reporting of strange atmospheres and peculiar feelings. Some other interesting, and perhaps less explainable, experiences have included the common sighting of a man dressed in green with a feather in his hat, who has been seen walking through a wall. Most of those who have claimed to witness this would not have known that this part

Above and right: *Highwayman, Sourton.*

of the pub used to be the way to walk to the stable block! This figure may be a man named Samuel, a Cavalier who apparently died during a battle and cannot leave the inn. Intriguingly there was in fact a historic clash at Sourton Cross during the Civil War, and the Royalists suffered an unsatisfactory defeat. I visited the inn and the surrounding area near to the anniversary but sadly had nothing of real interest to report.

Inside the pub is a very eye-catching door which was claimed from the shipwreck of a boat called *The Diana*. Several members of the crew perished. Some have claimed that the sailors' lost souls may now haunt the Galleon Bar, especially the captain named Bill. It is perhaps disappointing that no highwaymen are reported to haunt the pub, though they did apparently frequent the area in the past.

Other ghosts who allegedly frequent the Highwayman Inn include a monk and a lady in a mob cap, though why a monk would be haunting this building is unclear.

Branscombe's Loaf

High on Sourton Common is Branscombe's Loaf – a small rocky hill said to have once been visited by the Devil himself and so named as a result of the story attached to it. The Bishop of Exeter, one Walter Branscombe, (who died in 1280) is said to have once got lost here in the mist on his way to Tavistock. He became severely hungry and uttered the words, '…I would give anything for a bite to eat'. Suddenly there appeared a mysterious cloaked old man, who proceeded to offer the bishop some bread and cheese. As the bishop stretched out his hand to accept this kind offering, his accompanying chaplain swiftly spotted that the strange gentleman's feet were cloven and that he was somewhat skeletal in appearance. He shouted out a warning that the Devil himself was under the cloak and the bishop pulled his hand away – the bread and cheese dropping to the floor – and the evil one vanished without trace. The dropped food allegedly turned to stone and still stands on the hill to this very day.

Tavistock

Abbey

A number of buildings remain to mark the old abbey in Tavistock. The most charming is Court Gate, an archway leading from Bedford Square. This was the main entrance to the Great Courtyard of the abbey. A section of the cloister wall and other parts still stand in the churchyard and nearby. Betsy Grimbal's Tower, a ruined gatehouse, is situated in the garden of the vicarage, near the Bedford Hotel. Inside the archway is a stone tomb (unearthed in the eighteenth century), believed to house the remains of Abbot Ordulf, a supposedly giant monk dating from Viking times (977AD).

The tower is said to be haunted by a local lass lured here by a sailor in the 1700s. He had his wicked way before murdering the unfortunate girl. Many people have described a feeling of uneasiness, eeriness, melancholy and fear and even feelings of being watched within the area, and the apparition of a young girl has also been seen. People have reported camera failure and other electrical problems here.

However, the best-attested ghost is that of Betsy Grimbal herself, apparently murdered by either a jealous monk or, in some stories, a soldier. The slaying occurred in the tower; perhaps on the spiral staircase, where her bloodstains have intermittently appeared. She (or the other girl, as both stories seem to be interlinked and confused) has also been seen looking from a window, often as a prelude to a disaster. In Bedford Square itself, people have reported seeing a fleeting glimpse of ghostly monks walking along the street or in the tunnels underneath.

Bedford Square, Tavistock.

Torquay

Penny's Cottage

In early 2002 I was a member of GRFI (The Ghost Research Foundation International) and received a phone call from its president Jason Karl asking if I would be willing to assist in an investigation at a property in south Devon. This transpired to be Penny's Cottage, an absolutely delightful fifteenth-century thatched former Saxon longhouse divided into two separate living areas. I duly investigated both sites on the 23 March 2002, along with my friend Alan Maxted and two other GRFI investigators; the medium Paula Phelps and her husband Gary. I have honestly never seen such a unique building, rumoured to embrace underground tunnels connected to the local abbey at Torres and an underground well, and I felt very privileged to be investigating it.

The house and the hill above it get their name from John and Peggy Penny, who lived there in the early part of the nineteenth century. In 1894 Penny's Cottage was sold at auction, not as a single dwelling but as three separate ones. It was not until about 1950 that the three dwellings were converted into one house. Old pictures show a bare-sided valley where the rock features are clearly seen. Before we arrived I was given some background information about the activity, and I was simply amazed at how much there was.

Firstly, there were apparently two children who died here in a fire whose crying and voices have been heard on numerous occasions. A ginger cat has been seen and assumed, by most, to be a real pet, at least until it suddenly vanished. I was told the property was also haunted by a sea captain and his parrot, a doctor (who was related to the captain) and a bluebell dancer named Sylvia. The actor Terry Scott (of *Terry and June* fame) had apparently lived here at one time, and I will to my shame confess to immediately having mischievous thoughts about the possibility of ghostly echoes of 'oh June' reverberating around the walls. I am pleased to report this didn't happen! I also learnt that footsteps are often heard, that animals frequently 'play up' and, most remarkably of all, pennies often appear in places, seemingly out of nowhere. This was apparently associated with the former owner and the person whose surname the cottage is named after, a certain Peggy Penny.

Penny's Cottage, Torquay.

When we arrived we met the generous owners Maureen and Donald Phillips and prepared for the investigation by setting up and placing control (trigger) objects around the building. Due to the nature of past reported phenomena we decided to place coins (pennies) around in significant locations around the building to distinguish if they would be moved. We then set up locked-off cameras and swiftly began the investigation.

The experiences we all had that night were widespread and in many cases difficult to explain. In fact I feel I can honestly say that paranormal activity did in all probability occur, as we could almost certainly rule out human interference for much of what later happened. The first strange activities related to olfactory phenomena; firstly four of us smelt strong tobacco, then, all of a sudden, it was like sweet pipe smoke. Nobody was smoking and no windows were open. A few minutes later, we could perceive the smell of roses; this in a building empty of flowers. This was followed by a repeat of the tobacco incident.

We were invited to attempt dowsing in order to look for the position of the well; I had certainly not previously had any idea where it was positioned. To my surprise, I accurately discovered the correct location, and then others did as well. This was strange for me because before and since I have had very little success with dowsing and am well known for my failings in the discipline.

The next unexplainable occurrence happened at about 10.50 p.m., after the group had gathered to carry out a séance. Paula made apparent contact with Peggy Penny, who spoke with a slight West Country accent and appeared to be a gentle soul. She then expressed that she wanted to show us a strong sign of her presence and would do so by moving the control objects (coins). As soon as we broke the séance Alan, Gary and myself headed straight off to check the coins (which had been thoroughly checked just before the séance) and resultantly discovered that two different coins had moved by a significant amount. As the other participants joined us and we were looking at the coins, Donald actually claimed to see a coin moving in front of his eyes. The areas had been secured and so almost certainly no human interference was possible, and vibration aspects and other building-contributory factors were ruled out.

Soon after this, two people heard clear footsteps in the other part of the building, where nobody was present. We then began another séance at 11.55 p.m., and placed sound-recording equipment in the centre of the circle. Paula re-established contact with Penny and she promised to do something even more significant. At exactly midnight the recording equipment suddenly switched off. This had never happened before on any investigation previously and I still have this equipment today and it has never failed like this again. I checked the batteries afterwards and the mechanisms, all of which were fine. It was very peculiar, as was the whole night, and one of my most memorable investigations ever. I can honestly state that Penny's Cottage made quite an impression on me, and was one of the few places that I have come away from feeling that I simply could not explain events. I wondered if I'd ever get the chance to return.

Then, in May 2005, something terrible happened. An arsonist, twenty-one-year-old Tony Norman, set fire to the thatched cottage and it was completely destroyed. It appeared to be the end of this grandiose building, which had stood for so many centuries. Then, at the end of last year, I received an email from a friend of mine, Laura Oakes, who had experienced a strange incident and wondered if I could shed any light on it. Here is her correspondence (copied with Laura's kind permission):

Hi Ian,
I am really sorry to trouble you, hope you are well?
I feel a little daft but I have to tell you what happened to me last week. I went to visit a relative

in Devon and we had a day out in Torquay. While there he showed me a house that had recently burned down and commented on the shame of it, as it was very old and had a lot of history, anyway while he was talking my head went very fuzzy and I felt quite sick, and a woman's voice came into my head saying that she had a message for Ian, you are truthfully the only Ian that I know, so I can only assume that it is for you, she said her name was Peggy then she said she was called Penny so I am a bit confused but she definitely said both names. Anyway she said the walls are burning but I am still here and that when a shell is put back you have to go back again, and that you have to believe now don't you Ian. I hope this makes some sense to you if not I will try to rack my old brains and see if I can find someone else called Ian but at the minute you are the only one that I can think of.
Many thanks
Let me know if it means anything to you please, as I'm deadly curious
Laura

I am sure Laura would have had no idea about the fact I had ever been here and so when I replied this is what she said in return:

So you were there then at some time? That has made me feel very uneasy, as it has never happened before. I have had feelings and thoughts but never a voice with a message. I hope there is something that you can do about it, and why did she say you have to believe now did that make any sense to you? I think I need a lie down now. I get a little too thoughtful about things sometimes and at the moment I am wondering how on earth (or otherwise) did this lady relate me to you in anyway and why not through my brother who is more in tune with this kind of thing than I am.

I do believe in all things until its proved otherwise and like most people I would like to know the truth and I guess I will get used to things like this happening, because the images and things that I get are getting stronger and more frequent but at this moment I would have felt better if you told me you knew nothing about it, daft eh! When I read those pages you sent I was seriously freaked out, but now I feel a little privileged.
Thanks you for taking the time to answer
Many best wishes
Laura

Very interesting stuff! Laura had not experienced this type of thing previously and I feel I know her well enough to trust her! So I cannot explain this in any easy way. At face value it would appear to be an incredibly intriguing development.

Then I discovered in the local press that plans were being made to reconstruct the blackened shell of Penny's Cottage, turning it back into its former glory with specialist restoration work, replacing those features consumed by fire with contemporary materials. This work was almost complete as I started writing this book and, in April 2006, I made an impromptu visit to take a look and found the new building to be very similar to how it had looked previously, a testament to some very hard efforts and expert work. Long may it survive!

I will confess that the above comments from Laura were on my mind as I walked around the exterior and spoke briefly to the new owners. However I did not get the opportunity to enter inside and so, as of yet, I am not too sure as to why I should have returned unless it was just to see the new construction, which made me feel very content. Since the investigation, both Donald Phillips and Alan Maxted have sadly passed away – R.I.P.

Spanish Barn, Torquay.

Torres Abbey, Torquay.

Old Spanish Barn

Built in 1196 by the monks of Torre Abbey, this building was used in July 1588 to imprison 397 prisoners of war from the Spanish Armada. Their galleon, the *Nuestra Senora del Rosario*, had been towed to Torquay and the crew (including Don Pedro de Valdés, one of the main commanders of the armada) were placed inside the barn in very cramped conditions. As a result, very few survived; most of them died of illness and disease. One of the prisoners transpired to be a young woman who had been smuggled aboard the ship. She also died, and was given the last rites by a priest. However, this seems not to have laid her spirit to rest because her ghost is now believed to haunt the area near to the tithe barn. Remarkably, people driving past have seen a beautiful Mediterranean girl drifting slowly back towards the entrance of the barn or into the surrounding park, with a very down and tired-looking face; after a while she disappears.

A very interesting Victorian painting called 'The Surrender' shows the capture of this ship by Sir Francis Drake on 30 July 1588; it is on display at Buckland Abbey.

Torres Abbey

The abbey itself was built in 1196 and by the fifteenth century was the wealthiest Premonstratensian monastery in England. For eight centuries it has housed the abbots, Lords of the House and the mayors of Torquay, but at the time of writing the grand doors have closed until 2008, while an extensive six million pound makeover of this scheduled ancient monument is carried out. The gatehouse is fourteenth century, and after the dissolution of the monasteries this building was a residential house from 1539. Since 1930 Torbay Borough Council has owned it.

The Cary family owned this for much of the previous period and Lady Cary, who was a socialite in the 1770s, is rumoured to haunt this location. She is either seen walking on foot or riding in a carriage, resplendent in a ball gown. As she moves she appears to emanate a shimmering bright light.

In the Long Gallery people have heard footsteps from unseen feet. No person could be in the area to make these sounds when they occurred. Many people sense feelings of being watched or of not being alone and others talk of feelings that something unpleasant may have occurred here. This may relate to a fourteenth-century-break-in by a mob. On 20 November 1351 Richard de Cotelforde was claiming his right to be the new abbot, and due to disagreements his supporters broke in and committed assault, vandalism and theft. For his troubles Richard was later murdered by the brother of his rival abbot, Geoffrey Gras, who later was remarkably pardoned by the King.

Other things to happen in the abbey include doors slamming and other unknown sounds.

Totnes

This is undoubtedly one of my favourite Devonish towns and, according to locals, has more than its fair share of ghostly activity, but then it is also claimed to be the second oldest borough in the country! It is primarily an Elizabethan town with much to see.

Bay Horse Hotel

On an inclined street near the town centre, the inn is an attractive place, bedecked with window boxes and said to date back as far as 1485. It has a traditional vibe, though is also bright, jovial and atmospheric. A man wearing a red coat is said to haunt the pub. He is small in stature and elderly and has been seen on a number of occasions. He usually disappears very quickly and only certain people seem able to see him, while at the same time others are completely unaware that he's there. A few years ago a customer also claims to have been staying in one of the guest rooms when she was awoken by a strong feeling of being watched and could make out a man with a straw hat moving across the room. He disappeared almost immediately and was not seen again.

Castle

This fine Norman castle, with imposing views over the town, probably dates from the eleventh century, but has been added to and rebuilt on various occasions. It is now one of the best-preserved shell keeps in the country. However, little remains of the original motte and bailey castle, which was made of layers of earth, rock and clay crammed down onto a natural rock pile, with a wooden tower on its crown. In the early thirteenth century a stone shell keep was added

Bay Horse Hotel, Totnes.

Totnes Castle.

to the summit of the motte and it became one of the first three stone castles in Devon, and stone walls were constructed around the bailey below. It is said that visitors have heard voices and cries and yet, when they've turned around, there is nobody there. I must confess when I visited the castle, knowing this claim, I was intrigued to hear cries from the high point myself and wondered if I was about to have a supernatural encounter. Disappointingly it transpired to be some children playing behind the summit! An American lady became extremely spooked when she visited the castle and immediately had to leave. Overall though, Totnes Castle seems to be tranquil in comparison to most such fortresses, which perhaps stands to reason as it saw relatively little action over the years.

Guildhall

The Guildhall on Ramparts Walk is a well-preserved sixteenth-century structure. The building was constructed in 1533 on top of the ruinous Benedictine priory and still serves as a council chamber. Visitors to the Guildhall can see the table where Cromwell sat in 1646 during the Civil War, and Totnes' Old Jail where many psychic impressions of sadness have been reported. There is no definitive ghost here but it is more about impressions, feelings and atmospheres – which are almost tangible. The classic 'feelings of being watched', cold temperature drops and sudden impressions of being unnerved or not alone are all experienced here! In particular, an area leading via a stairway to the council chamber is an active area for this type of feeling, though the feeling of dread approaching a council chamber could undoubtedly be a common occurrence at many locations across the country! One visitor did report that a caretaker who lived on the premises had told her that he had seen a woman sitting in a chair one morning. He said his hair stood up on end as this woman 'shimmered' away and then disappeared, and he positively believed he had seen a ghost. The building has been used as a courthouse, a school and as a ceremonial meeting place.

Kingsbridge Inn

Situated at the top of the town on Leechwell Street, this seventeenth-century inn has a long tradition of providing a warm welcome, excellent food and good ale. The bar has a wonderful 'olde-worlde' appearance, with a classic open fire, old wooden beams, brass lamps, an old pump that used to draw waters from Leech Wells and plenty of nooks and crannies. The inn has an intriguing history and was once claimed to have been the regular of liquor smugglers.

The pub has apparently been haunted for a very long time and as long as anyone can remember. In the seventeenth century barmaid Mary Brown was apparently seduced by a former landlord and then raped and murdered, legend later claiming that he entombed her body in the walls. Her ghost is apparently only seen by female customers, particularly at the top of some stairs, in the bar, the pump room or the kitchen. She is described as being tall, with dark hair tied in a bun. Some people have described her as being hazy in appearance whereas others have described her as solid. A medium visiting once also picked up the presence of a former landlady named Sarah Taylor. Interestingly records do show a Sarah Taylor as residing here in the 1830s. Also another previous landlady was seen sitting in a chair (now removed) in the pump room.

Other more general experiences at the inn have included the sudden drop of temperatures in various parts of the pub, strong feelings of being watched and dogs who suddenly start to act up, growling at some unseen thing. The nearby Leech Wells are said to be haunted by a White Lady and to be full of healing qualities – hence they were a place of pilgrimage for lepers.

Museum

Almost certainly one of the finest restored Elizabethan town houses in the country. This fascinating museum was built in about 1575 for a wealthy local cloth merchant. The museum contains many exhibits highlighting local history and there is also a local history study centre. It is said to have a resident spook, usually sighted in the Victorian grocery shop, who is described as little more than a vague misty form.

Above left: *Guildhall, Totnes.*

Above right: *Kingsbridge Inn, Totnes.*

Right: *Totnes Museum.*

Priory Gatehouse

The gatehouse to the Benedictine priory once stood in what is now Fore Street. The priory was founded in 1088 by Juhel of Totnes as a cell of St Nicholas's Abbey at Angers. Its buildings, like so many, were demolished soon after the Dissolution. However, in about 1540, during times of wealth, a house was built on the site, possibly incorporating parts of the gatehouse. It has been claimed that a young girl of that era haunts the property. As is similar in many places there is a reported 'atmosphere' and sudden temperature drops. However there have also been some poltergeist activities as well. Items are often found to have moved or been replaced, this occurring while nobody can have been present.

St Mary's Church

This church is a fine-looking construction in the early perpendicular fashion. A soaring 120 foot high tower, containing eight bells, is situated at the west end. In 1799 a pinnacle was struck by lightning and fell through the porch roof. This led to the discovery of two chests full of ancient records, from which it appeared that the church had been rebuilt in 1259, and again in 1432, but the earliest records showed a Norman construction here in 1066. A Grey Lady is said to haunt the churchyard and also the adjacent Ramparts Walk. She is described as appearing to almost glide, and is seen wearing Elizabethan costume. We can only hope that this is not simply somebody wandering home from the market. Since 1970 a group of local traders have clothed themselves in Tudor costumes on Tuesdays, throughout the summer, to commemorate the town's prosperity during this historic time.

South Street

I had previously read in the excellent book *Ghosts of Totnes* by Bob Mann a story about a ghostly swan (a one-footed one at that!). This bird is said to haunt this area of Totnes and so, during a visit to the town, I made some enquiries. I eventually had a conversation with a charming elderly couple who lived in the street and who directed me to a particular cottage formerly known as Swansfoot. It has now been renamed but was apparently previously haunted by a swan. People would hear beating wings at night and a swan's foot was found hidden in the recess of a wall. There were also local reports of a ghostly swan which would fly in at night from the River Dart and land on the cottage roof. Apparently no activity has occurred in the house in recent years. However, I have learnt that a swan had been seen in the street a few weeks previously. Whether or not this was spectral would of course be hard to substantiate!

William IV Hotel

A cook named Bill (who used to work, and indeed died, here) allegedly haunts this inn, situated in the historic main street. He is described as an elderly gent and mostly appears in the upper rooms of the pub. The building has previously been victim to strange poltergeist occurrences, such as electrical problems and mysterious moving objects. This has all been blamed on Old Bill (not the police, I hasten to add!).

Two Bridges

The Two Bridges Hotel

Situated beside the West Dart River in the very midst of the Dartmoor National Park and by the famous picturesque two bridges, The Two Bridges Hotel is indicative of a bygone age of wealth. Built in 1794 as a coaching inn, the building was originally called 'The Saracen's Head'. It only gained its present name in the early 1900s, with the modern road being completed in 1931. Guests have frequently smelt old-fashioned perfume and felt a sudden chill in the air in a certain room; a couple from London recently described having a very scary night here at the hotel though they failed to give specific details.

Above left: *Totnes church.*

Above right: *Two Bridges Hotel, Dartmoor.*

Right: *William Hotel, Totnes.*

Above and left: *Jay's Grave (kindly provided by Kevin Hynes).*

Widecombe-in-the-Moor

Jay's Grave

This is undoubtedly one of the most quoted ghost stories there is, and in summary the history of the site is as follows: lying on a crossroads off the B3344 is a turf-covered rectangular grave with a rough headstone. It is almost always covered in freshly cut flowers and foliage and this is part of the legend. Back in the late eighteenth century an orphan named Kitty (or Mary) Jay was seduced by a local farmer and fell pregnant. The shame led to her committing suicide at the fresh age of about sixteen. She did this in a barn at either Ford or Canna's Farm and, as was traditional, her body was buried at this crossroads in an unhallowed last resting place. Custom was inclined this way because it was believed that people should do this in order to confuse the spirit, which would then be unable to find its way back to 'civilisation'. In 1860 the site was disturbed and a young girl's skeleton discovered. Subsequently the bones were reburied and the grave erected as it stands today. It is claimed that nobody knows who places the flowers there but in truth it is probably a self-fulfilling prophecy. The wider-known the story the more likely people are to visit the site and place flowers, perpetuating the myth.

There have also been sightings at night of a dark, hooded figure in long dark clothing bending over the grave in a state of sorrow and grieving. The form is seen for a short time before vanishing. In 1978 a lady went on local television and went into a trance where she claimed to be a milkmaid called Kitty Jay who had been made pregnant by a farm labourer at Canna Farm on Dartmoor and had hanged herself in a barn. This lady supposedly had no prior knowledge of the story, and when she was taken to the actual farm she became very distressed. She seemed to have an uncanny prior knowledge of the layout of the place.

In May 2006 some friends of mine from PRO carried out an all-night vigil here, and described it as 'cold, windy and dark … and not much else!', although two independent investigators picked up on the same spirit presences, and once it went dark the atmosphere around the grave did change remarkably.

Old Inn

The Old Inn, where 'Uncle Tom Cobley and all had a few ales on their expedition to Widecombe Fair on Tom Pearce's grey mare' is set in the heart of the beautiful Dartmoor countryside. The inn was built in the fourteenth century and lies right in the centre of the village, opposite the church. The Old Inn retains much of the original stonework and fireplaces and burns real log fires; it is therefore perfect for a cold winter night on Dartmoor.

The haunting is said to involve a crying baby and a man who walks through an upstairs wall.

The crying has been blamed on an unseen child who haunts one of the bedrooms upstairs. Yet when anyone opens the door to enter the wailing immediately stops. At times it has persisted all night and been heard by countless individuals. This pub also has the ghost of 'Old Harry', who is seen to walk between the kitchens and the bars. This older gentleman reportedly walks the ground floor of the public house, fading away when he reaches the kitchen. Harry may have been murdered here, and his most active time seems to be mid-afternoon.

Old Inn, Widecombe.

One thing of immense interest is the fact that the inn had a very bad fire in 1977, which resulted in the part of the inn where the paranormal activity was being extensively rebuilt. The landlord said that the ghosts have not been seen or heard since (for twenty years), and there is little evidence of widespread haunting activity today.

St Pancras Church

This beautiful Gothic structure is often referred to as 'the cathedral of the Moor', and the church dates back to the fourteenth century. The main story about the church refers to a devastating storm that occurred on Sunday 21 October 1638. The church tower was struck by lightning and a ball of electricity entered the church itself. As a result, four people and a dog were killed, and sixty people injured. A legend claims that this carnage was enacted by the Devil himself as he came to collect the soul of one Jan Reynolds, a notorious local gambler and sinner. Others who were killed included Roger Hill, Robert Meade and also the minister; George Lyde's wife was badly injured. As the massacre occurred, many claimed to have smelt fire and brimstone, and others even claimed that the Devil himself appeared, grabbed Jan, and rode away on the back of his jet-black horse. Allegedly the Dark Angel had also been seen earlier at the Tavistock Inn ordering a pint of ale and asking for directions to Widecombe. These stories are almost certainly a superstitious reaction to such a terrifying occurrence in God's own house, although there is a story of a phantom horseman at nearby Hemsworthy Gate.

Hemsworthy Gate

A dark horseman clothed in a military-style uniform is said to ride at speed along the road at Hemsworthy Gate which leads from Ashburton to Widecombe, though others have claimed that the phantom is actually that of a coach and horses. He moves swiftly but silently on moonlit nights and is claimed by many to be the ghost of a highwayman! Some witnesses have even suggested that the spirit is headless as he rides across the track. Perhaps this is even less likely than the claim that the Old Grey Mare from the Widecombe Fair folktale now haunts the streets of Widecombe. The beast is heard, rumour has it, rattling along on the eve of Widecombe Fair, and appears in a cloud of blue light.

Wonson

Northmore Arms

After driving around Dartmoor visiting various haunted locations I decided to head for the Northmore Arms in the village of Wonson, near to the villages of Throweigh, Gidleigh and Chagford. I had heard various stories about the place and so felt the trip through the slender country lanes would be well worth it. After encountering several near misses on the incredibly narrow walls over a bridge – where past paintwork scrapings were all too apparent – I arrived in the small car park and headed towards the pub. I was immediately struck by the solitude and remoteness of this place and felt that the chances of anyone being at the pub were remote. However within seconds of me leaving my car a local man with a fine looking black Labrador and a stout walking stick passed me on my journey to the door. I soon learnt more than I expected about this captivating tavern – apparently it is haunted by a sailor.

Northmore Arms., Wonson.

My first reaction to the claim that an old-fashioned sailor with bushy beard haunts the pub was one of incredulity. After all, the pub is many miles from the sea on either coast. However, it transpires that this road was part of the Mariner's Way, and sailors leaving one ship at, say, Dartmouth in the south would travel across land to join another ship in the north of Devon. It was easier to travel across land than to take the treacherous route around the coast of Devon and Cornwall. Therefore the story is perhaps not as unlikely as one would first suspect, and it would seem that several unsuspecting visitors have described seeing the same image over a long period of time.

Wonson Manor

The Northmore Arms are named after the Northmore family, who owned the manor for many years. Sections of the house are said to date back to the twelfth century, however, it was extensively renovated and restyled in the seventeenth century. One particular member of the family, and lord of the manor, was a certain William Northmore, renowned gambler and eccentric. On one infamous occasion it was said he lost a huge amount of money on the turn of a card. Subsequently he painted the ace of diamonds (the card in question) in his room and would often be found swearing and cursing at it. Indeed some claim he still haunts the building to this day. In the same bedroom unseen hands have tucked people away in bed and smoothed a pillow.

A slightly differing story describes four seventeenth-century Cavaliers who have been seen playing cards, an apparent playback of when William managed to gamble away his riches. However as William was not born until 1690, and the consensus is that this gambling defeat occurred in 1722, I am not sure if this can realistically be an authentic story. Interestingly enough, the year 1722 is when William registered the Northmore Coat of Arms, still seen on the side of the Northmore Arms to this day!

REFERENCE/SOURCE BOOKS

A Companion to the Folklore, Myths and Customs of Britain – Mark Alexander
Celebrity Ghosts of Devon – Mike Holgate
Classic Devon Ghost Stories – Paul White
Dark & Dastardly Dartmoor – Sally and Chips Barber
Devon Ghosts – Theo Brown
Devon Mysteries – Judy Chard
Ghastly and Ghostly Devon – Sally and Chips Barber
Ghost Hunting South West – Michael Williams
Ghostly Encounters South West – Peter Underwood
Ghosts & Hauntings – Dennis Bardens
Ghosts of Devon – Peter Underwood
Ghosts of North Devon – Peter Underwood
Gothick Devon – Belinda Whitworth
Great Ghost Hunt – Jason Karl
Guide to Ghosts and Haunted Places – Peter Underwood
Haunted Britain – Anthony Hippisley-Coxe
Haunted Castle of Britain and Ireland – Richard Jones
Haunted Castles – Mark Ronson
Haunted Dartmoor: A Ghost Hunters Guide – R.W. Bamberg
Haunted Happenings in Devon – Judy Chard
Haunted Inns of Britain & Ireland – Richard Jones
Haunted Pubs in Devon – Sally and Chips Barber
Place Names in Devon – Chips Barber
Souvenir Book and Guide – Combe Martin Wildlife and Dinosaur Park
Strange Stories from Devon – Rosemary Anne Lauder and Michael Williams
Strange West Country Hauntings – Graham Wyley
The Encyclopaedia of Ghosts and Spirits – John and Anne Spencer
The Ghosts of Berry Pomeroy Castle – Deryck Seymour

REFERENCE/SOURCE BOOKS

The Ghosts of Brixham – Graham Wyley
The Ghosts of Exeter – Sally and Chips Barber
The Ghosts of Totnes – Bob Mann
The Haunted Pub Guide – Guy Lyon Playfair
West Country Hauntings – Peter Underwood
Weird and Wonderful Dartmoor – Sally and Chips Barber

Other haunted titles published by Tempus

Haunted Brighton
ALAN MURDIE

This fascinating book contains a chilling range of supernatural phenomena, from the ghost of Cary Grant at the Rottingdean Club to the Screaming Skull in the Lanes and the ghost who spelt out 'prove me innocent!' at Preston Manor. Containing séances, spirits, cellars and spectral hands, this scary selection of ghostly goings-on is bound to captivate anyone interested in the supernatural history of the area.

0 7524 3829 8

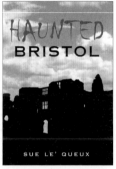

Haunted Bristol
SUE LE QUEUX

This selection of newspaper reports and first-hand accounts recalls strange and spooky happenings in Bristol's ancient streets, churches, theatres and public houses. From paranormal manifestations at the Bristol Old Vic to the ghostly activity of a grey monk who is said to haunt Bristol's twelfth-century cathedral, this spine-tingling collection of supernatural tales is sure to appeal to anyone interested in Bristol's haunted heritage.

0 7524 3300 8

Haunted Cornwall
PAUL NEWMAN

For anyone who would like to know why Cornwall is called the most haunted place in Britain, this collection of stories of apparitions, manifestations and related supernatural phenomena from around the Duchy provides the answer. *Haunted Cornwall* includes chilling tales and first-hand encounters with phantoms and spirits who haunt prehistoric graves, and is sure to delight ghost hunters everywhere.

0 7524 3668 6

Haunted Winchester
MATTHEW FELDWICK

Including tales of spectral monks at Winchester Cathedral and phantom horses in Cathedral Close, haunted landmarks and the Eclipse Inn where Dame Alice Walker, condemned by the hanging Judge Jefferies, still walks, *Haunted Winchester* is sure to captivate anyone interested in the supernatural history of the area.

0 7524 3846 8

If you are interested in purchasing other books published by Tempus, or in case you have difficulty finding any Tempus books in your local bookshop, you can also place orders directly through our website

www.tempus-publishing.com